CW01176564

gothic
dark glamour

gothic
dark glamour

Valerie Steele and Jennifer Park

Yale University Press and The Fashion Institute of Technology New York

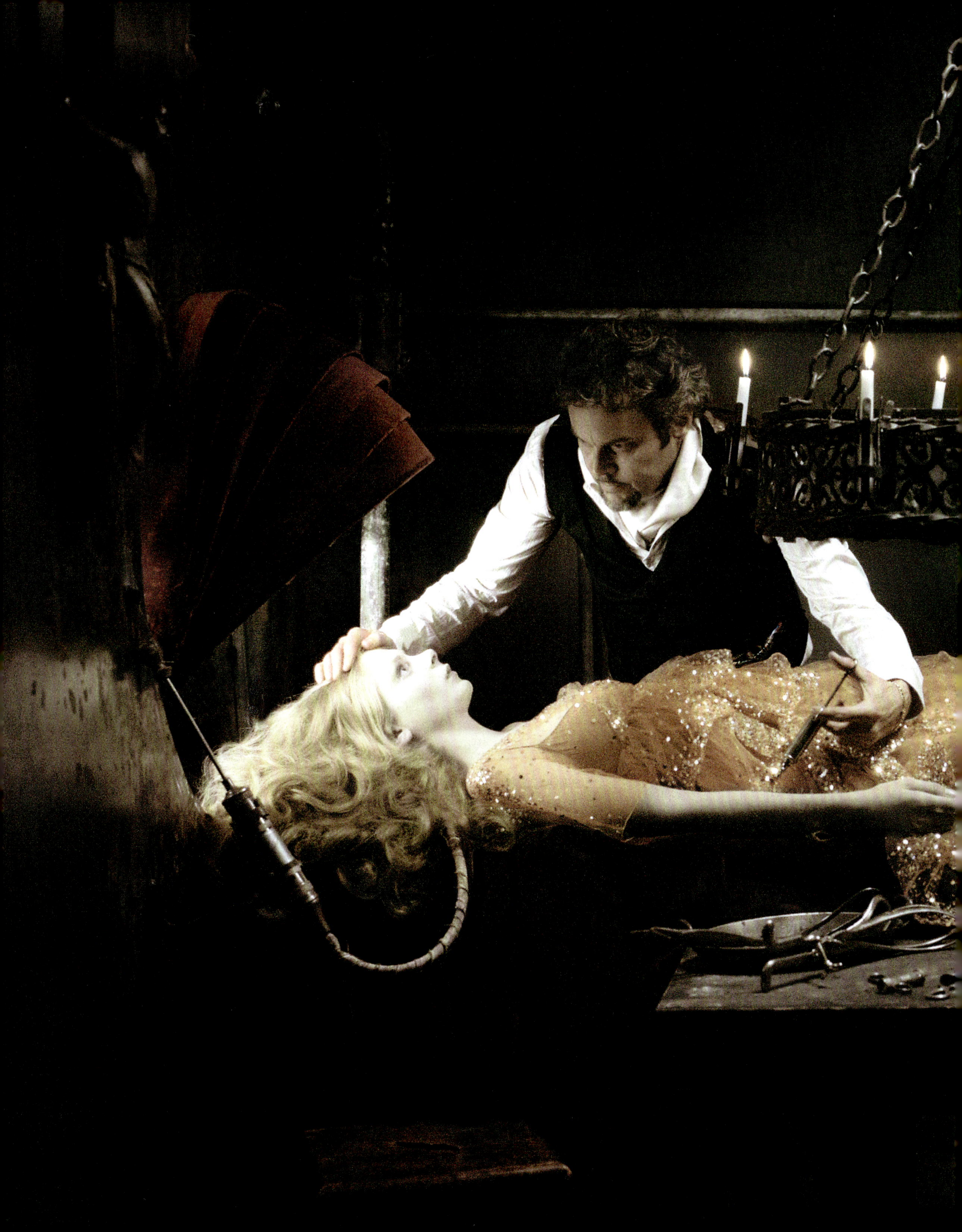

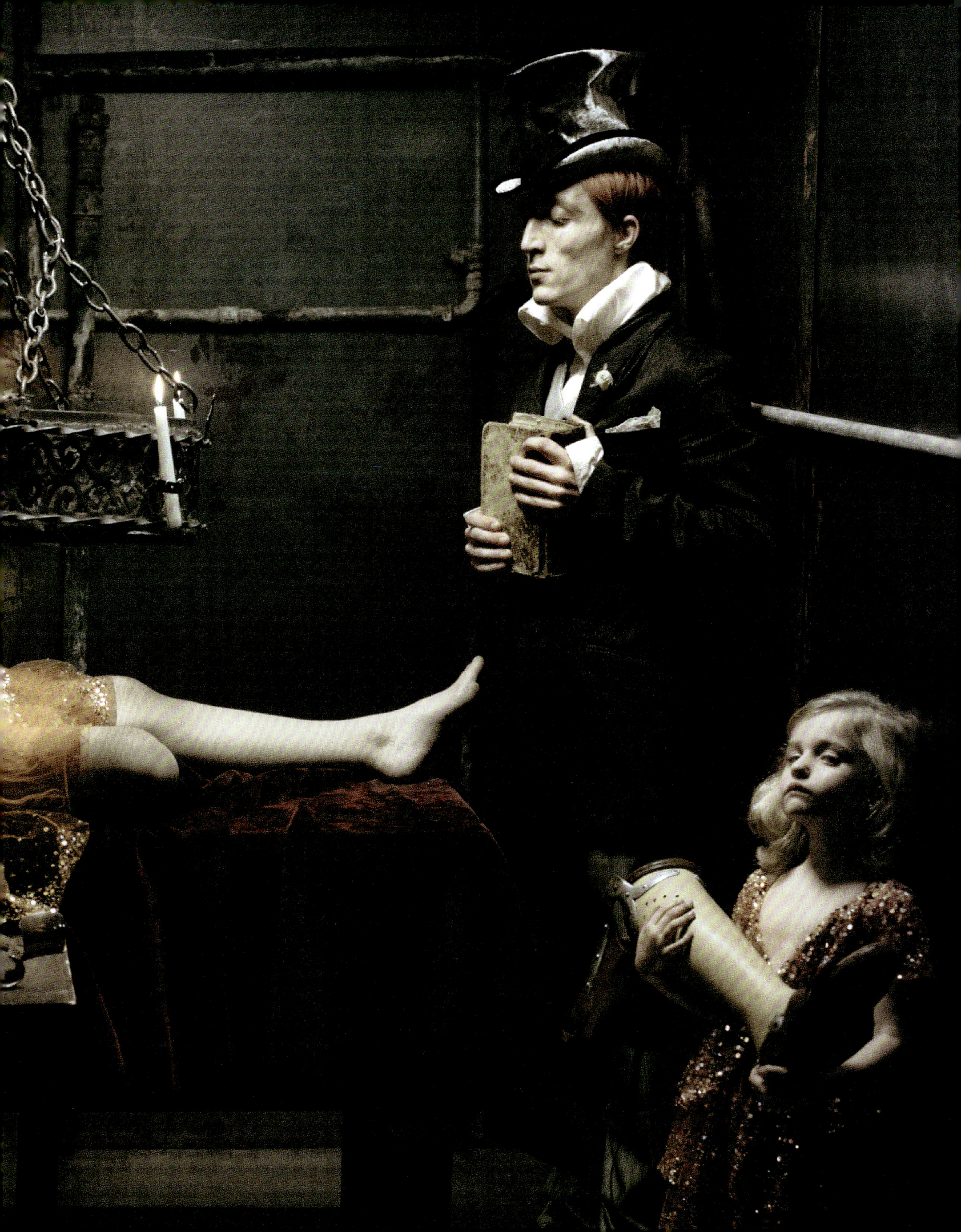

This book is dedicated to Colleen Hill for her invaluable assistance

Designed by Paul Sloman

Printed by Conti Tipocolor

Library of Congress Cataloging-in-Publication Data

Steele, Valerie.
 Gothic : dark glamour / Valerie Steele and Jennifer Park.
   p. cm.
 Includes bibliographical references and index.
 ISBN 978-0-300-13694-4 (cl : alk. paper)
 1. Gothic rock music--Social aspects. 2. Goth culture (Subculture) 3. Fashion. I.
Park, Jennifer, 1977- II. Title.
ML3918.G68S74 2008
306'.1--DC22

                         2008024961

P. IV. Untitled, from "Les Costumes," *Madame Figaro*, 2006. Photograph courtesy Eugenio Recuenco, represented by Gianfranco Meza & Co.

P. VIII. Untitled, *Stern,* 2005. Photograph courtesy Eugenio Recuenco, represented by Gianfranco Meza & Co.

contents

Acknowledgements	x
Gothic: Dark Glamour	1
Melancholy and the Macabre: Gothic Rock and Fashion	115
Select Discography	166
Select Bibliography	169
Select Electronic Resources	172
Index	174

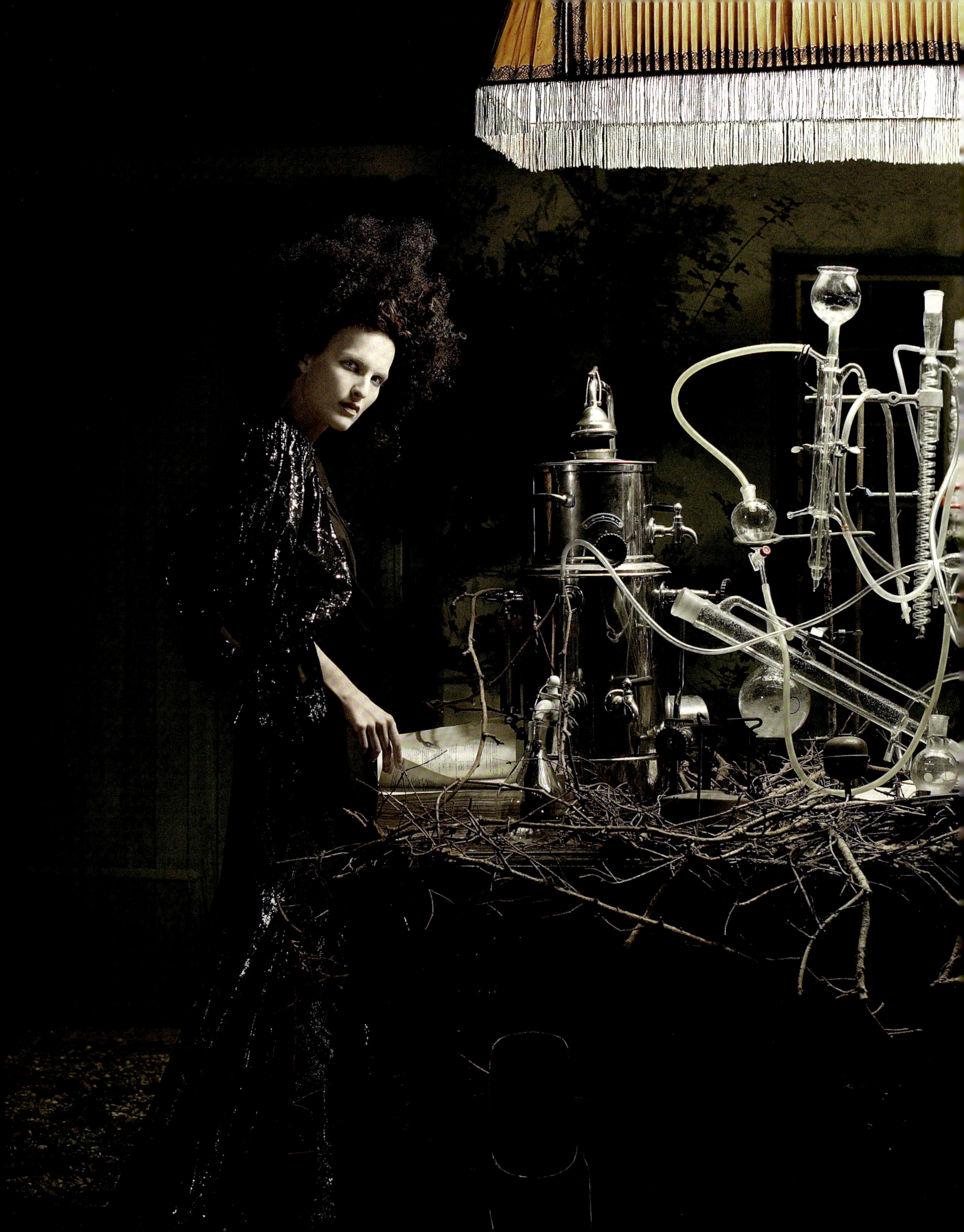

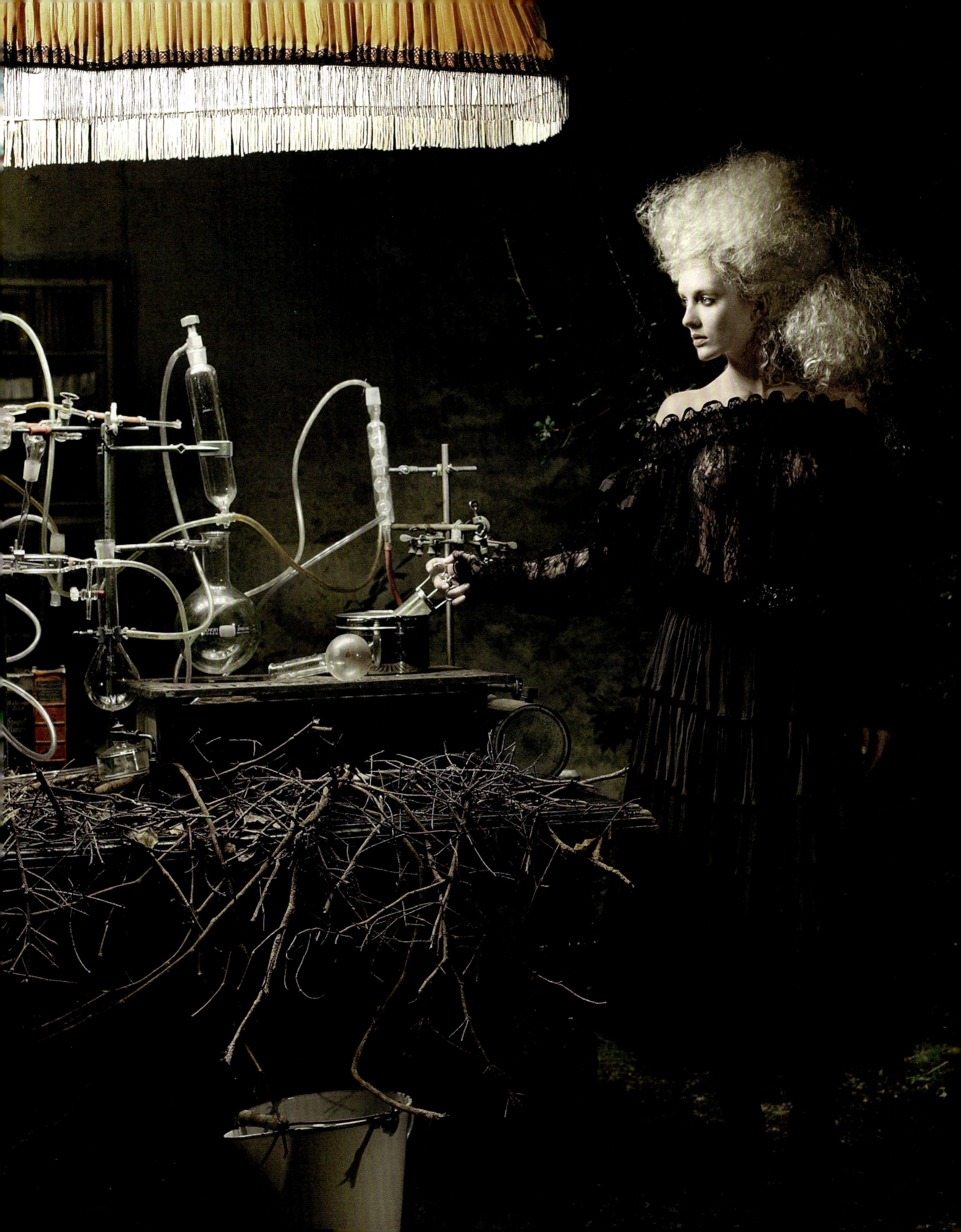

acknowledgements

Many people helped make this book possible. In particular, we would like to thank the designers, artists, photographers, musicians, and goths who allowed their works to be featured and/or allowed us to quote from interviews conducted in the course of writing this book. Special thanks to Aiden Aldred of Alexander McQueen, Anne Babel, Carole Barlot, Antonio Barrella, Beggars Banquet (Kathryn Braddick and Steve Webbon), Jennifer Belt, Abby Bennett, Fred Berger, Elisabeth Bonnel, Julia Borden, Kat Bret, Barry Briggs, Trevor Brown, The Burns Archive (Elizabeth and J-Sun Burns), Eric Charles, Isabelle Chalard, Hussein Chalayan, Judith Clark, Tomás Clusellas, Condé Nast Publications (Leigh Montville), Simon Costin, Les Cyclopes (Damien Beneteau and Xavier Cariou), Neil Francis Dawson, *Dazed & Confused* (Sylvia Farago and Nicola Formichetti), Ann Demeulemeester, The Detroit Institute of Art (Sylvia Inwood), Simon Doonan, Kayte Ellis, Sean Ellis, Fashion Group International, Dan Fox, John Galliano, Atelier Gattinoni (Edoardo de' Giorgio), Perry Hagopian, Pandora Gorey Harrison, Freya Horn, Indexcommunications, The International Center of Photography (Erin Barnett, David Seidner Archive), Martina Hoogland Ivanow, Kambriel, Pat Kerr, Yasunari Kikuma, Angela Kim, King Features Syndicate (Susan White), Jon Klein, Shaun Leane, Ariane Lemee, Mandi Lennard, Roxanne Lowit, Andrew Macpherson, Laura McCutchan, John Major, Tanya Marcuse, Maison Martin Margiela, Andrea Martin, Mick Mercer, The Metropolitan Museum of Art (Eva Peters and Teresa Romito), Gianfranco Meza, Evan Michelson, Thomas Miller, Pamela Mills, Chris Moore, Dennis Morris, Patricia Morrison, Thierry Mugler, Kate and Laura Mulleavy of

Rodarte, The Museum of the City of New York (Phyllis Magidson and Chris Murtha), Jelka Music of John Galliano, The National Museums Liverpool (Nathan Pendlebury), Claudio Napolitano, Rick Owens, Christopher Park, Soizic Pfaff of Christian Dior, Colleen Piano, Plastik Wrap (Ryan Webber), Ted Polhemus, Gareth Pugh, Housk Randall, Eugenio Recuenco, Samuel Rooker-Roberts, Zoë Roberts, Paolo Roversi, Peter Saville, Angelika Schubert, Aaron Sciandra, Rieko Shibazaki, Jody Shields, Jordan Shipenberg, Justin Smith, Reynolds Smith, Steve Spon, Anna Sui, Shoko Takayasu, Yeohlee Teng, Olivier Theyskens, Ruben Toledo, Max Vadukul, Steven D. Valentine, Maria Chandoha Valentino, Anne van den Bossche, Stefan Verresen, Victoria and Albert Museum (Stephanie Fawcett), Mariano Vivanco, *Visionaire* (Cecelia Dean and Dominic Sidhu), *Vogue Nippon* (Gene Krell and Kiori Okamoto), Dita von Teese, Christine and Nicholas Wade, The Walker Art Gallery, Mark Walsh and Leslie Chin, Jane Wildgoose, Karen Wright, The Lewis Walpole Library at Yale University (Susan Walker), Nancy Wong, Carla Wachtveitl and Alexis Brooks of Yohji Yamamoto, Naomi Yoda, and Masayuki Yoshinaga.

Since this book accompanies a major exhibition at The Museum at FIT, a number of people at the museum provided significant assistance, including Varounny Chanthasiri, Julian Clark, Ann Coppinger, Fred Dennis, Jill Hemingway, Colleen Hill, Julie Lin, Amy McEwen, Patricia Mears, Carmen Saavedra, Tamsen Schwartzman, Irving Solero, Tommy Synnamon, Vanessa Vasquez, and Stefan Verresan. As always, it is a pleasure to work with Gillian Malpass and her colleagues, Katharine Ridler and Paul Sloman, at Yale University Press.

gothic

ent
dark glamour

Valerie Steele

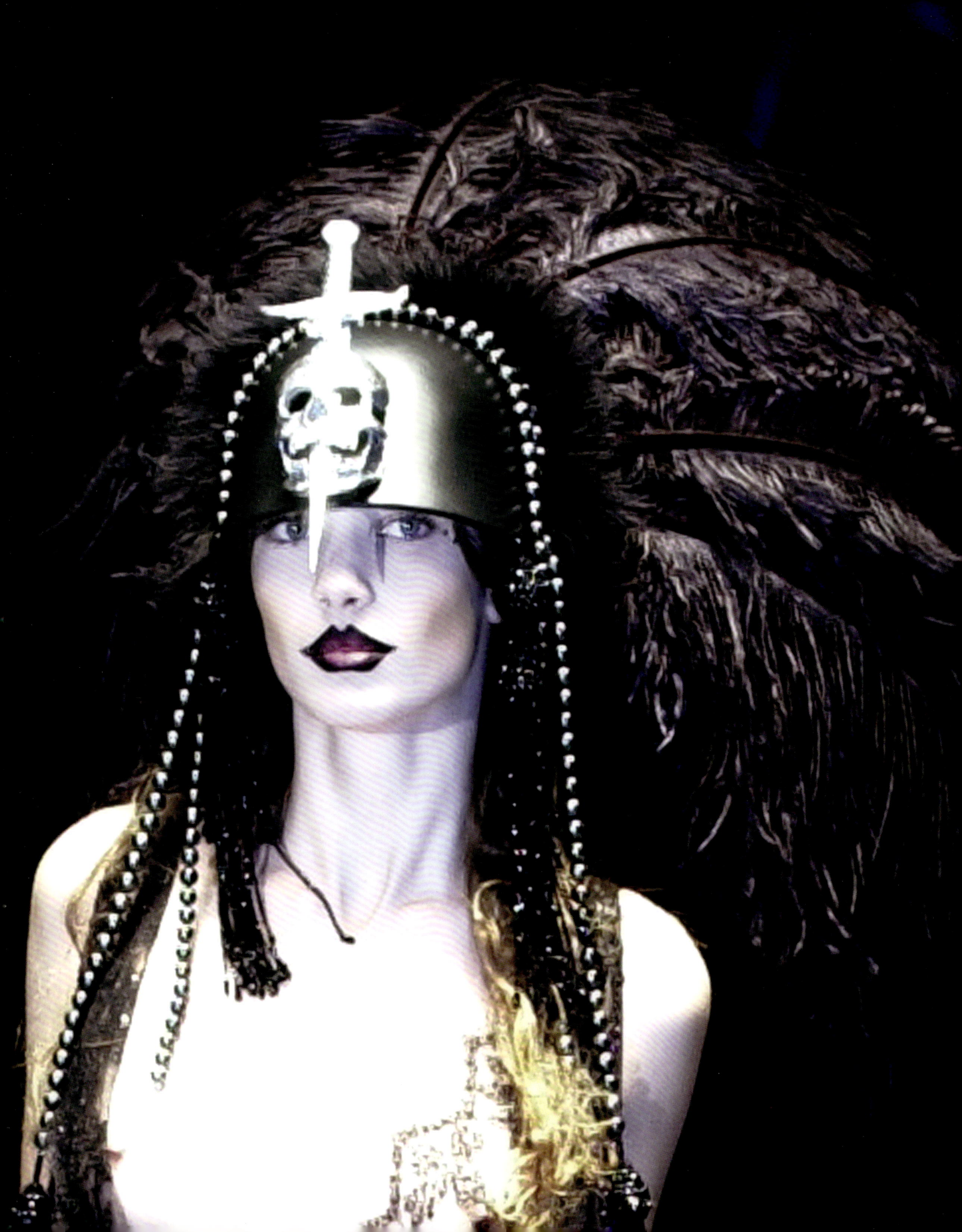

G"Gothic" is an epithet with a strange history, evoking images of death, destruction, and decay. It is not just a word that describes something (such as a Gothic cathedral), it is also almost inevitably a term of abuse, implying that something is dark, barbarous, gloomy, and macabre. Ironically, its negative connotations have made it, in some respects, ideal as a symbol of rebellion. Hence its significance for youth subcultures. Today the words "goth" and "gothic" are popularly associated with black-clad teenagers and mascara'd rock musicians. But the gothic has many layers of meaning.

1. Alexander McQueen Fall/Winter 2001/2. Photograph courtesy Chris Moore.

Although there have been innumerable studies of the gothic in literature, cinema, art, and architecture, surprisingly little has been written about the gothic influence on fashion. Yet the gothic look has been an important, recurring theme in contemporary fashion, not only within the goth subculture, but in high fashion as well. Alexander McQueen, John Galliano, Rick Owens, Olivier Theyskens, and Yohji Yamamoto are among the many designers who have created what could be interpreted as gothic fashions, whether or not they would accept that label — some probably would not, because the gothic is vulnerable to being dismissed as a morbid or kitsch style.

So what is "gothic fashion"? Why is it so often maligned? What is the source of its enduring appeal? This essay will attempt to answer these questions. Most

2. Limbourg Bros. (fifteenth century). May, calendar miniature from *Les Très Riches Heures du duc de Berry*, 1416. Courtesy Réunion des Musées Nationaux/Art Resource, NY.

studies of the gothic begin with the etymology of the word itself, which derives from the Latin *gothicus*, "of or pertaining to the Goths" (*gothos*), a nomadic, warrior people inhabiting the forests of northern Europe in the third century AD. The Romans regarded Germanic tribes like the Goths and Vandals as barbarians. This image was definitively established when the Visigoths sacked Rome in AD 410, triggering the fall of the Roman Empire. Later, another tribe, the Ostrogoths, repeatedly invaded Italy, destroying the aqueducts and decimating the population. Henceforth, the Goths were notorious for "carrying Destruction before them as they advanced, and leaving horrid Deserts every where behind them," as Edmund Burke wrote in 1752.[1] Yet as this quotation from Burke implies, by the eighteenth century there was already thought to be something "sublime" about the wild and dangerous Goths.

3. Hans Holbein the Younger, *The Dance of Death*, 1538. Woodcut.

The gothic story picks up again in the Middle Ages, when a new style of art and architecture developed in northern Europe. Gothic cathedrals were characterized by soaring spires, pointed arches, flying buttresses, and stained-glass windows. Although much admired today as the expression of medieval piety, cathedrals such as that at Chartres were disparaged in the early modern period, when the style was retroactively termed the Gothic (from the Italian *gotico*, "rough, barbarous"), because it was different from both ancient classical architecture and the modern Renaissance aesthetic. Bodies, like buildings, were gothicized. As depicted in medieval art, the Gothic nude had a slender, elongated body, quite unlike the classical nude that inspired Renaissance artists. This stylization of the body in art reflected the lines of medieval fashion.

The European Middle Ages saw the beginning of fashion as the term is generally understand today – as a regular pattern of style change. Traditional costume historians use the term "gothic fashion" to describe northern European medieval dress from the thirteenth through the fifteenth centuries. Gothic fashion was form-fitting yet exaggerated, with long trailing sleeves and extraordinary head-dresses. Ladies' dresses featured shockingly deep décolletage, while young men wore skin-tight leggings, long pointed shoes, and short doublets decorated with pinking, slashing, and lacing. Yet medieval art was not all chivalry and elegance. When the Black Death decimated the population of Europe, it spawned a macabre obsession with skeletons and rotting corpses.

Just as the barbarian Goths were the dark Other of classical civilization, so also the medieval Gothic came to be viewed as modernity's Other, its "dark side." With the rise of the Enlightenment, the entire medieval period was retrospectively envisioned as the Dark Ages, characterized by superstition and religious fanaticism, when an irrational fear of witchcraft, sorcery, and Satanism ran rampant. As such, the Gothic proved perversely attractive to certain cultural outsiders, such as the homosexual aesthete Horace Walpole, who not only built a little "Gothick" castle but also wrote the first Gothic novel, *The Castle of Otranto* (1764), which inaugurated a vogue for melodramatic horror stories with titles such as *The Monk* and *The Mysteries of Udolpho*. Architectural ruins especially suited the new taste for romantic, backward-looking thoughts, and Protestant England had many ruined monasteries and crumbling churches. In their absence, picturesque, new Gothic Revival "ruins" could be constructed. Meanwhile, the gothic literature of terror was characterized by gloomy settings (such as ruined castles), mysterious, violent, and supernatural events, and a general atmosphere of degeneration and decay.

Tracing the genealogy of the gothic sensibility leads one down peculiar historical

4. Louis Daguerre, *Ruins of Holyrood Chapel*, 1825. Oil on canvas. © Walker Art Gallery, National Museums, Liverpool.

pathways, where the "fatal women" and "corpse passions" of the Romantic and Decadent movements take on a new life. Gothic literary studies tend to focus on iconic English novels, ranging from Mary Shelley's *Frankenstein* (1818), in which a monster is artificially created in a sinister laboratory, to Bram Stoker's *Dracula* (1897), in which a foreign vampire aristocrat wreaks havoc in Victorian England. Romantic novels, such as *Wuthering Heights* and *Jane Eyre* (both 1847), established an enduring neo-gothic genre featuring dangerous yet strangely attractive men who threatened innocent young women. However, as a genre, the gothic draws also on French Decadent literature, German Expressionist cinema, and the Hollywood horror film, the last of which, especially, was crucial in establishing the visual iconography of the gothic.

The most important contemporary manifestation of the gothic is the goth subculture, which developed in the late 1970s. Goths were associated both with a new style of music (dark) and a new style of dress (overwhelmingly black). An outgrowth of the punk subculture, goth also drew on the trappings of gothic literature and film, such as vampire movies, medieval religious iconography, and Victorian mourning customs. Goth's greatest period of popularity was in the early to mid-1980s, but the subculture never disappeared and it experienced a significant revival in the late 1990s. Although fashion journalists tend to denigrate it, designers and stylists have periodically been strongly influenced by goth subcultural style.

Post-punk bands such as Bauhaus popularized an image of black-clad goths which continues to influence mainstream fashion almost thirty years later. The September 2007 issue of American *Vogue*, for example, included a two-page fashion spread on "Goth" as part of its supplement *Fashion Rocks*. Photographed

5. (left) Pandora Harrison, 1996. Red satin with black lace overlay corset by True Grace England, bat detail necklace from Siren of Toronto. Photograph: Housk Randall. Courtesy Pandora Harrison and Housk Randall.

6. (right) German Goth at the Last Cathedral club. Berlin, 2007. *WWD Fast.* Photograph: Matti Hellig. Courtesy Fairchild Archive © Condé Nast Publications Inc.

7. (following page) Masayuki Yoshinaga's portrait of Rie. Reproduced from *Gothic & Lolita*, published by Phaidon Press Limited © 2007 Phaidon Press Limited, www.phaidon.com. Courtesy Masayuki Yoshinaga.

8. (page 9) Alexander McQueen Spring/Summer 2003. Photograph courtesy The Fashion Group Foundation.

PLATINUM
2006.11/11@CLUB NEO
OSAKA EVERY 2nd SATURDAY HIPHOP PARTY!
ULTRA NANIWATIC MC'S & DJ FUKU
DJ ケンイチ
DJ KIREW / DJ YOGA / DJ USK / DJ AKTION
KOM'S & AMI
HE CURSE OF
SPECIMEN

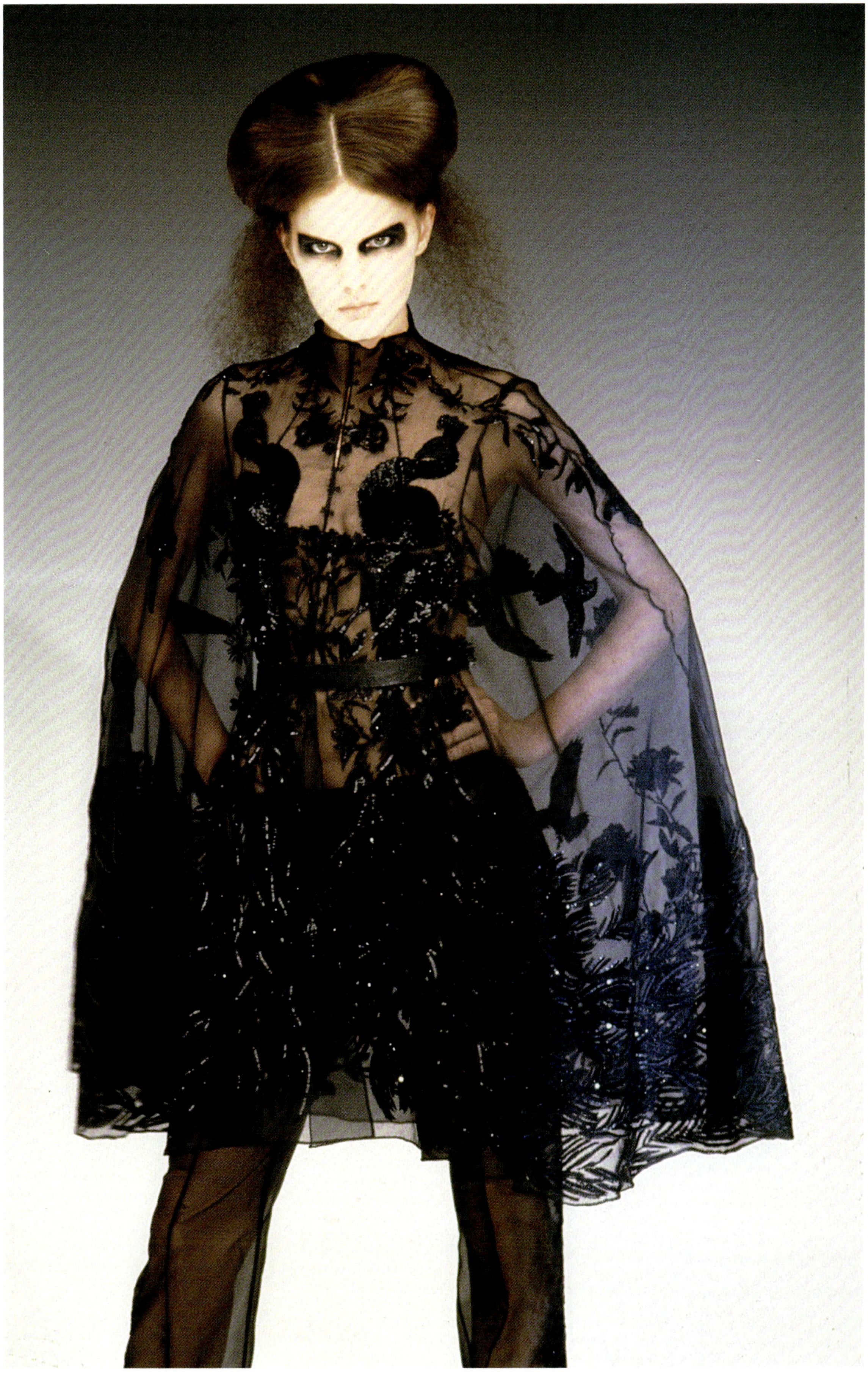

by Steven Meisel, the models were styled to look like goth musicians with extreme maquillage and black hair. Featured were looks by John Galliano for Christian Dior (Poison gown and Neptune jacket) and by Alexander McQueen (dress and boots), as well as dresses by Christopher Kane, Giles, and Calvin Klein. The text explained: "They say it began as an introspective, gloomy alternative to glossy pop tunes. Here, its drama is spellbinding, and its darkness is palpable."[2]

Although popularly associated with the goth subculture, gothic fashion encompasses far more than a single, historically situated subcultural style. It is not just that goth style has mutated over the years (from old-school goth to cyber-goth and beyond), but high fashion has also been "gothicized" in a variety of ways. Fashion journalists often describe a look as "gothic" simply because it is black, but this is deeply misleading. Although black is certainly the gothic color *par excellence*, for reasons that I shall explore, not all black clothes are gothic, nor is gothic fashion always black. For a fashion to be gothicized means that either the clothing itself or its representation in a fashion photograph or catwalk show alludes in some way to the vast pool of gothic associations.

9. Untitled, *Stern*, 2005. Photograph courtesy Eugenio Recuenco, represented by Gianfranco Meza & Co.

gothic narratives

> Costumes and disguises, veils and masks are ubiquitous features of Gothic fiction. From the giant helmet that falls on Walpole's Conrad in *The Castle of Otranto* (1764) to the costumes worn for contemporary Vampire Balls, clothing has always played a vital role in the construction of Gothic narratives.[3]

Beginning with the rise of the gothic novel in the eighteenth century, gothic style has been associated with sublime themes of terror and the supernatural. Death is central to the gothic imagination, but the gothic vision of death is profoundly ambiguous. Rather than definitively marking the end of life, death is inextricably intermingled with life, as revenants – ghosts, vampires, rotting corpses – constantly return from the dead.

Perhaps the first great image of gothic fashion is the ghostly white neoclassical nightgown worn by the swooning woman in Henry Fuseli's 1782 painting *The Nightmare*. An immediate sensation, *The Nightmare* was much parodied in its day and continues to be an icon of the gothic, because of its uncanny association of sex and death. The woman portrayed seems to hover in an indefinite state, somewhere between life and death. Has she fainted or expired? Is she having an orgasm or a seizure? Are the nightmare creatures oppressing her to be interpreted as supernatural beings or the products of her unconscious mind? Stories about vampires, demons, and witches were still widely believed during the eighteenth century, although educated people already dismissed them as superstitions. Yet as Fuseli observed, "We are more impressed by Gothic than by Greek mythology, because the bands are not yet rent which tie us to its magic."[4]

The scene depicted in *The Nightmare* is replicated in Ken Russell's delirious film *Gothic* (1986), in which Natasha Richardson plays Mary Shelley, wearing a closely similar white dress, recalling both a nightgown and a shroud. Other characters in the film play Lord Byron and Dr. Polidori, both of whom were associated with the novel *The Vampyre* (1819), as well as the doomed Romantic poet Percy Shelley. Thus, the film superimposes images from a variety of gothic narratives, literary, artistic, and biographical.

In his famous essay "The Uncanny" (1919), Sigmund Freud argued that certain sights arouse horror, because of an "uncertainty whether an object is alive or not." Especially uncanny subjects are "apparent death and the re-animation of the dead," which Freud associated with an infantile belief in the omnipotence of thoughts, wishes and fears. As rational adults, we think we have "*surmounted* these modes of thought; but . . . as soon as something *actually happens* . . . which seems to confirm the old, discarded beliefs, we get a feeling of the uncanny." It is as though we find ourselves thinking: "'So, after all, it is true that one can kill a person by the mere wish!' or 'So the dead do live on and appear at the scene of their former activities!'"[5]

The uncanny is "nothing new or alien," argued Freud, but on the contrary, "something which is familiar," which as been "repressed" and "which *recurs*."[6]

Thus, if we find something peculiarly frightening about pictures or dolls that come to life, doubles, haunted houses, and even the sense of *déjà vu*, it is because we are experiencing the return of the repressed. Although it is fashionable nowadays to dismiss Freud, his interpretation of the uncanny helps explain why the past hangs heavily over gothic narratives. It also underlines the psychological significance of supernatural phenomena.

Horace Walpole, briefly mentioned earlier, was one of the pioneers of both the Gothic Revival and the Gothic novel. Often depicted as the original goth, Walpole was the proud creator of a "little Gothic castle at Strawberry Hill."[7] There he wrote *The Castle of Otranto*, a supernatural tale of terror complete with multiple murders, ghosts and apparitions, a mysterious stranger, and a portrait that comes to life. Walpole was neither the first nor the last writer to exploit the macabre and supernatural. Shakespeare's *Hamlet* also features a castle, a ghost, a secret, madness, murder, and incest. Nevertheless, *The Castle of Otranto*, although

10. Henry Fuseli, *The Nightmare*, 1781. Oil on canvas. Founders Society purchase with funds from Mr. and Mrs. Bert L. Smokler and Mr. and Mrs. Lawrence A. Fleischman. Photograph © 2005 The Detroit Institute of Arts.

seldom read today, had an immense impact in its time. Following Walpole, "Monk" Lewis and Mrs. Radcliffe were other exponents of the "terrorist" school of literature whose lurid plots attracted a large public, setting the stage for a host of other sensational novels, stories, and films.

The Victorians despised Walpole. "None but an unhealthy and disorganized mind could have produced such literary luxuries as the works of Walpole," thundered the great English historian Macaulay. Walpole was "the most eccentric, the most artificial, the most fastidious, the most capricious of men. His mind was a bundle of inconsistent whims and affectations. His features were covered by mask within mask." Notice this emphasis on masking, which is relevant to the discourse on fashion. A homosexual and an aesthete, Walpole was an ambiguous figure, described by his most recent biographer as "the great outsider."[8] Yet it is precisely because of his peculiar "masked" status – the insider as outsider – that Walpole was able to create this extraordinary and highly artificial genre devoted to what

11. *Propaganda Gothic Chronicle*, no. 22 (Spring 1995). Photograph courtesy Fred H. Berger.

Shelley called "the tempestuous loveliness of terror." However, when Walpole saw *The Nightmare*, he pronounced it "shocking."[9]

In Walpole's day, classical architecture was said to be "rational," in contrast to the "licentious," "superstitious," "monstrous," "unnatural," and "deformed" gothic.[10] The diarist John Evelyn, for example, criticized Henry VII's chapel at Westminster for "its sharp *Angles*, *Jetties*, Narrow Lights, lame *Statues*, *Lace* and other *Cut-Work* and *Crinkle Crankle* . . . Clumsy Buttresses, Towers, sharp pointed Arches . . . Turrets, and Pinnacles . . . and abundance of busy Work."[11] Walpole loved the chapel. As he put it: "One must have taste to be sensible of the beauties of Grecian architecture; one only wants passions to feel Gothic."[12] When Walpole announced that he intended to "build a little Gothic castle," his friends initially disapproved, but Walpole insisted that he wanted to imprint "the gloomth of abbeys and cathedrals" on his house.[13]

The result, however, was more fanciful than gloomy, as Walpole and his "Committee of Taste" drew freely on a range of historical prototypes: a tomb in Canterbury cathedral inspired the fireplace at Strawberry Hill, while a choir

12. J. McArdell, after Joshua Reynolds, *Horace Walpole*, 1757. Courtesy the Lewis Walpole Library, Yale University.

screen in St. Paul's cathedral provided a source for the bookshelves. "My house is so monastic, that I have a little hall decked with long saints in lean arched windows," he wrote to Horace Mann. "Under two gloomy arches, you come to the hall and staircase . . . the most particular and chief beauty of the castle. Imagine the walls covered . . . [with] Gothic fretwork, the lightest Gothic balustrade to the staircase, adorned with antelopes (our supporters) bearing shields."[14] As Walpole himself admitted, "Every true Goth must perceive that they [the rooms at Strawberry Hill] are more the works of fancy than imitation."[15]

Walpole was among the first, but hardly the last, to embrace what came to be known as the Gothic Revival style. Although his fanciful little "Gothick" castle was essentially a rococo pastiche, architects such as A. W. N. Pugin and Viollet-le-Duc later attempted to achieve more historically accurate buildings. The gothic attracted a diverse array of personalities who looked to the past as a model for living. Medieval-minded Tories identified the style with tradition and legitimacy, while Whigs thought it evoked the freedoms enshrined in the Magna Carta. Like Walpole an enthusiast for trangressive medievalism, Sir Francis "Hell-Fire" Dashwood

13. Staircase at Walpole's Strawberry Hill, Middlesex, c. 1784. Courtesy the Lewis Walpole Library, Yale University.

founded his notorious club for libertines at the neo-Gothic Medmenham Abbey, where, dressed in monks' robes, the members of the Hell-Fire Club engaged in suitably sinful behavior far away from prying eyes.

English cultural nationalists approved of the gothic as a northern style in opposition to the classicism of France and Italy — although Gothic Revival architecture became popular also in France and America.

Although Strawberry Hill resembled a rococo stage set more than a genuine medieval castle, this was entirely appropriate for an eccentric aesthete such as Walpole, who once playfully received his guests "at the gates of the castle . . . dressed in the cravat of Gibbons's carving, and a pair of gloves embroidered up to the elbows that had belonged to James I. The French servants stared, and firmly believed this was the dress of English country gentlemen."[16] The stagey, even campy aspect of the gothic was there from the beginning and so, perhaps, was a homosexual subtext.

The inspiration for *Otranto* supposedly came to Walpole in a dream: "I thought myself in an ancient castle (a very natural dream for a head filled like mine with Gothic story) and that on the uppermost banister of a great staircase I saw a gigantic hand in armour."[17] Upon awakening, he began to write and in less than two months he had completed the entire novel. Initially, it was published anonymously and was alleged to be an actual medieval manuscript, but with the second edition Walpole came out as its author, adding the subtitle "A Gothic Story."

The story is too complicated to describe in detail, but in one famous scene, a monstrous helmet with sable plumes falls on young Conrad, heir to the house of Otranto, and crushes him to death in the courtyard of the castle. Conrad's father, the satanic, lustful prince Manfred, thereupon decides to divorce his wife and marry his dead son's destined bride, Isabella, who is forced to flee through "a labyrinth of darkness." The story reaches a climax when the castle crumbles into ruins: "What! Is she dead? cried he in wild confusion – A clap of thunder at that instant shook the castle to its foundations."

The supernatural would become increasingly associated with the psychological in later gothic narratives, such as Edgar Allan Poe's "The Fall of the House of Usher" (1839). Significantly, Poe specifies in passing that the house refers both to "the family and the family mansion." It may also evoke a mind degenerating into madness, an effect that Poe brilliantly creates in his horrific story of incest and premature burial, culminating at the moment when a "barely discernible fissure" in the House of Usher suddenly widens and the building collapses. Poe's iconic tales of horror also include "The Masque of the Red Death" (a plague story set in the Middle Ages) and his narrative poem "The Raven" (1945).

In *The Crimes of Love* (1800), the Marquis de Sade argued that gothic novels were "the fruit of the revolution of which all Europe felt the shock."[18] This is not entirely true, since the Terror of the French Revolution did not cause the novel of terror, although it probably contributed to the genre's growing popularity (Poe's story "The Pit and the Pendulum" certainly evokes the grisly image of death by guillotine). Yet Gothic style does not simply reflect social anxieties, since from the beginning it has been a knowing genre that plays with the pleasurable aspects of

14. "Lady Halcón," *Vogue Novias/Brides*, 2001. Photograph courtesy Eugenio Recuenco, represented by Gianfranco Meza & Co.

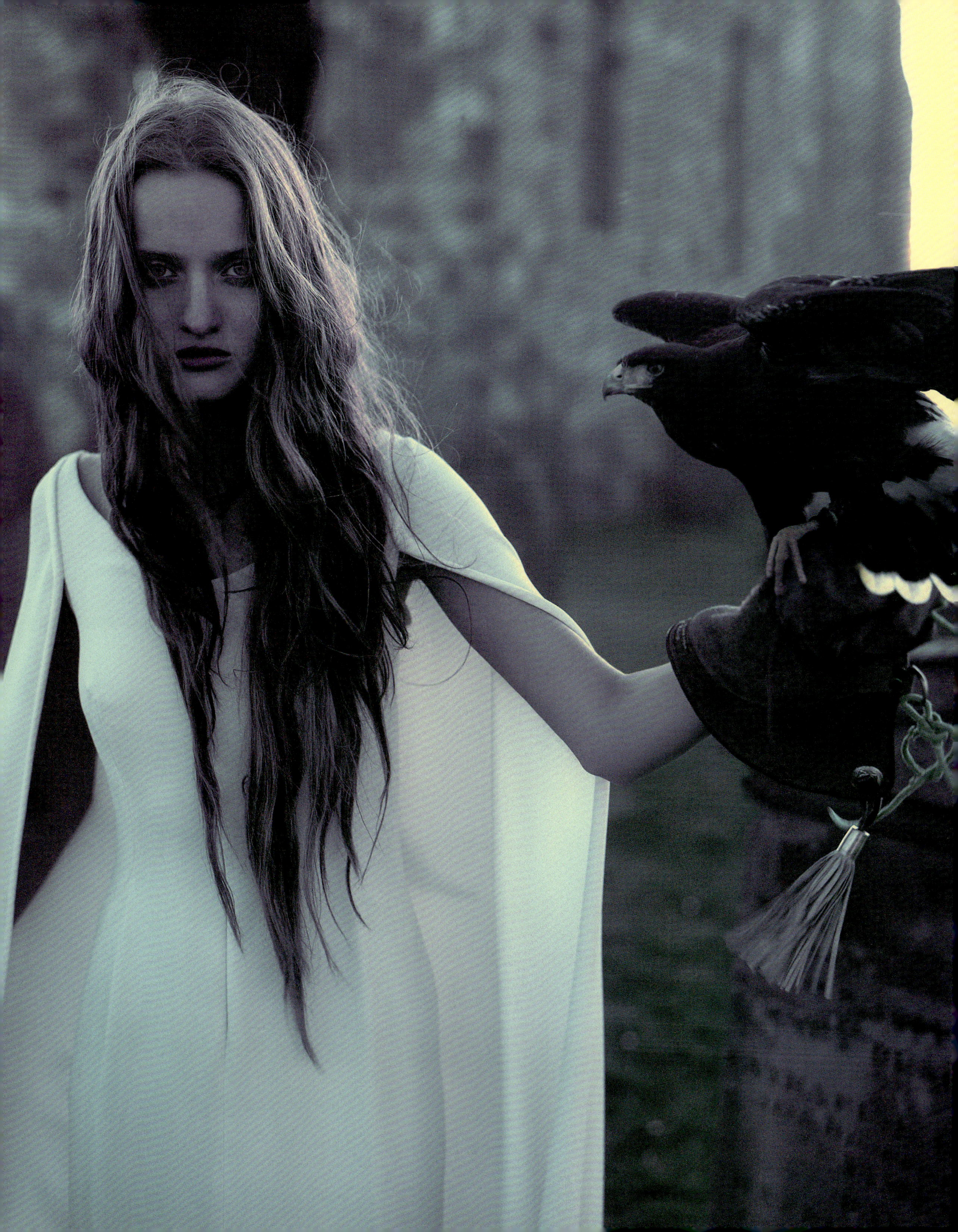

terror. The "divine marquis" was correct, however, in observing that the gothic is a modern genre, even when it draws on ancient fears.

The myth of the vampire, for example, is ancient and widespread. Fear of vampires was strengthened by the historical reality of bloodthirsty mass murderers, such as the fifteenth-century Vlad Dracul, known as Vlad the Impaler, and the Countess Bathory, the Blood Countess of Transylvania. Yet vampires only gradually moved from the margins to the center of the gothic imagination. Karl Marx described capital as dead labor, which, vampire-like, lives off the working class. The gothic novel, however, was primarily read by the bourgeoisie, who envisioned the vampire in the form of the feudal aristocrat.

Lord Byron, himself the very image of a wicked, sexy aristocrat, was influential in launching the fashion for vampires. The character of Lord Ruthven in Polidori's *The Vampyre* (1819) was inspired by Byron, whom Polidori knew, and it was initially believed that Byron himself had written the book, in which the evil and perversely fascinating Ruthven is killed in Greece, becomes a vampire, and murders his best friend's sister on the night after their wedding. However, it was not until Bram Stoker's *Dracula* was published in 1897 that vampires became central to modern popular culture. The erotic aspects of vampire fantasies are clearly foregrounded in passages such as the scene in which Stoker describes how Harker is surrounded by three female vampires:

> "He is young and strong; there are kisses for us all." I lay quiet, looking out under my eyelashes in an agony of delightful anticipation . . . The fair girl went on her knees and bent over me, fairly gloating. There was a deliberate voluptuousness which was both thrilling and repulsive, and as she arched her neck she actually licked her lips like an animal, till I could see in the moonlight the moisture shining on the scarlet lips and on the red tongue as it lapped the sharp white teeth. Lower and lower went her head as the lips went below the range of my mouth and chin and seemed about to fasten on my throat. Then she paused and I could hear the churning sound of her tongue as it licked her teeth and lips, and could feel the hot breath on my neck . . . I could feel the soft shivering touch of the lips on the supersensitive skin of my throat and the hard dents of two sharp teeth, just touching and waiting there. I closed my eyes in a langourous ecstasy and waited – waited with beating heart.[19]

Although Stoker highlighted the sexual subtext of vampirism, he ignored the question of appropriate costuming, merely observing that Dracula is "clad in black from head to foot, without a single speck of colour about him anywhere,"[20] while the female vampires have "the dress and manner" of "ladies."[21]

It was only with the rise of the cinema that the vampire's sartorial image came into focus. Bela Lugosi's appearance in Tod Browning's Hollywood film *Dracula* (1930) was especially influential. In some respects a stereotyped image of upper-class masculine elegance, purveyed to a mass audience during the Depression, Lugosi's formal evening attire (white tie) slightly modified Stoker's original vision of the Count in head-to-toe black. The costume also drew on historical and literary prototypes. Dracula's cape, for example, recalls Byronic images of masculinity,

15. *Visionaire* no. 7, *Black*, Fall 1992. Photograph by Max Vadukul. Courtesy Max Vadukul/Art Department and *Visionaire*.

16. (following page) Costume by Eiko Ishioka for Mina in *Bram Stoker's Dracula*, 1992. Photograph: David Seidner. ©International Center of Photography, David Seidner Archive.

17. (page 21) Costumes by Eiko Ishioka for the Vampire Brides of Dracula in *Bram Stoker's Dracula*, 1992. Photograph: David Seidner. ©International Center of Photography, David Seidner Archive.

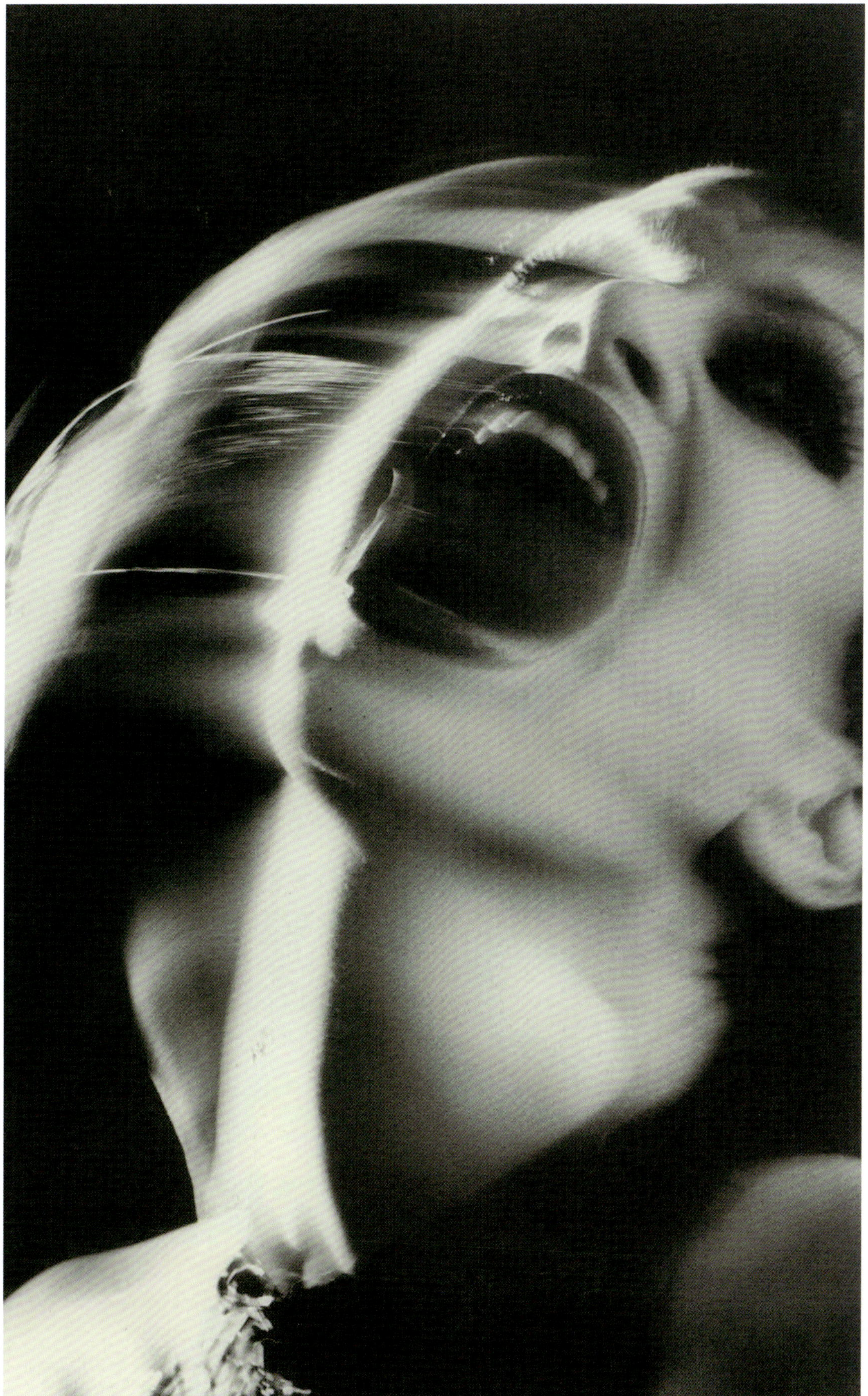

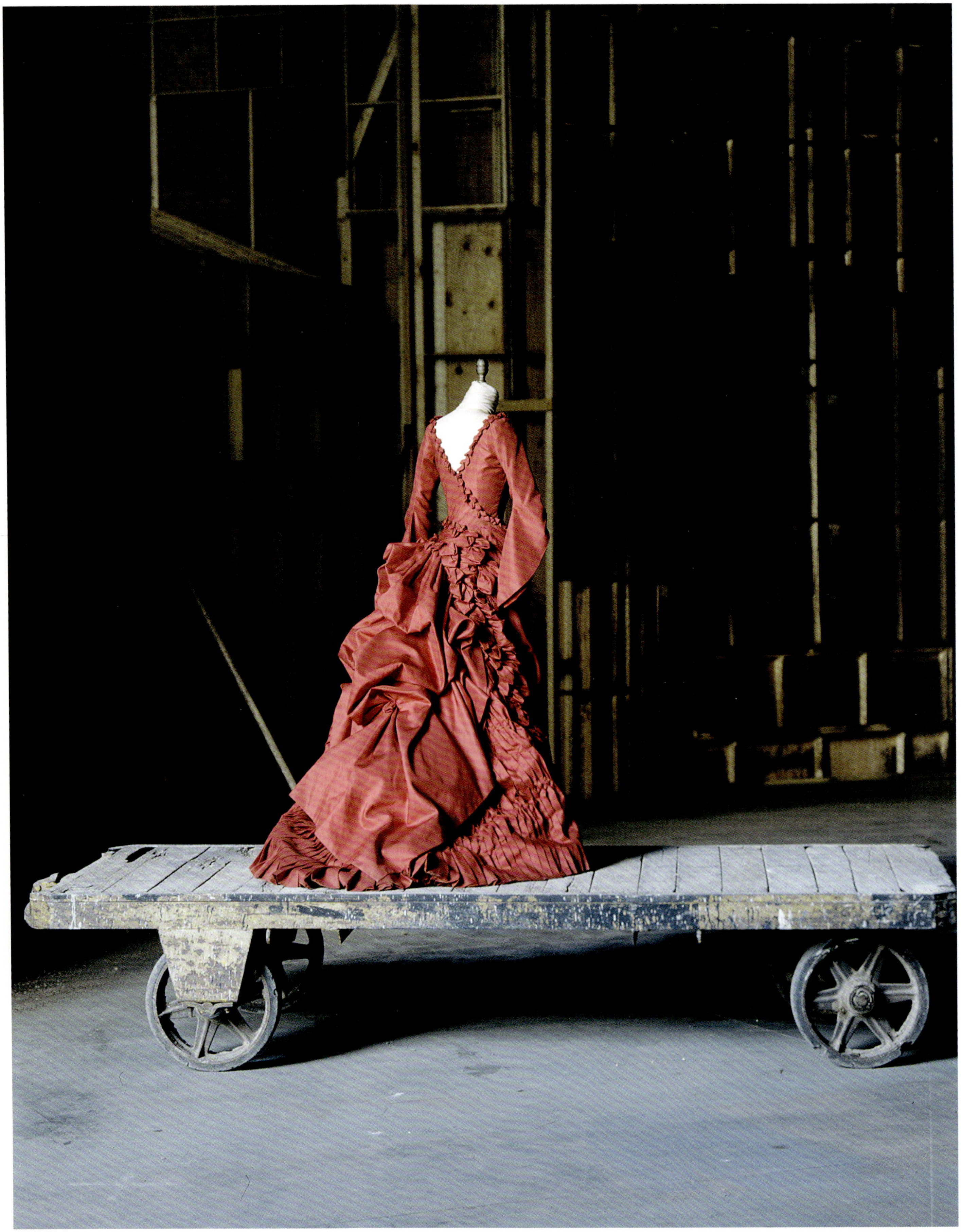

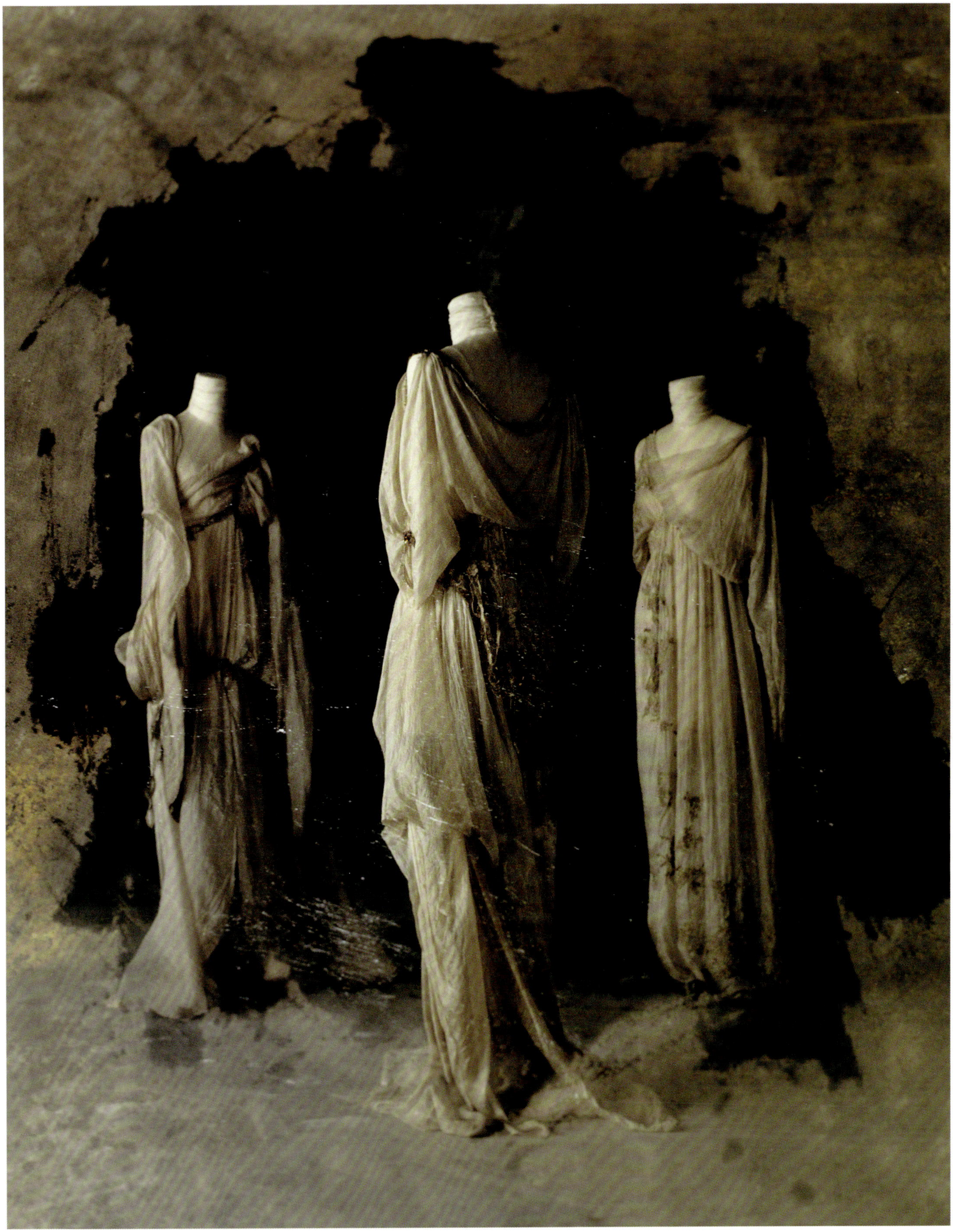

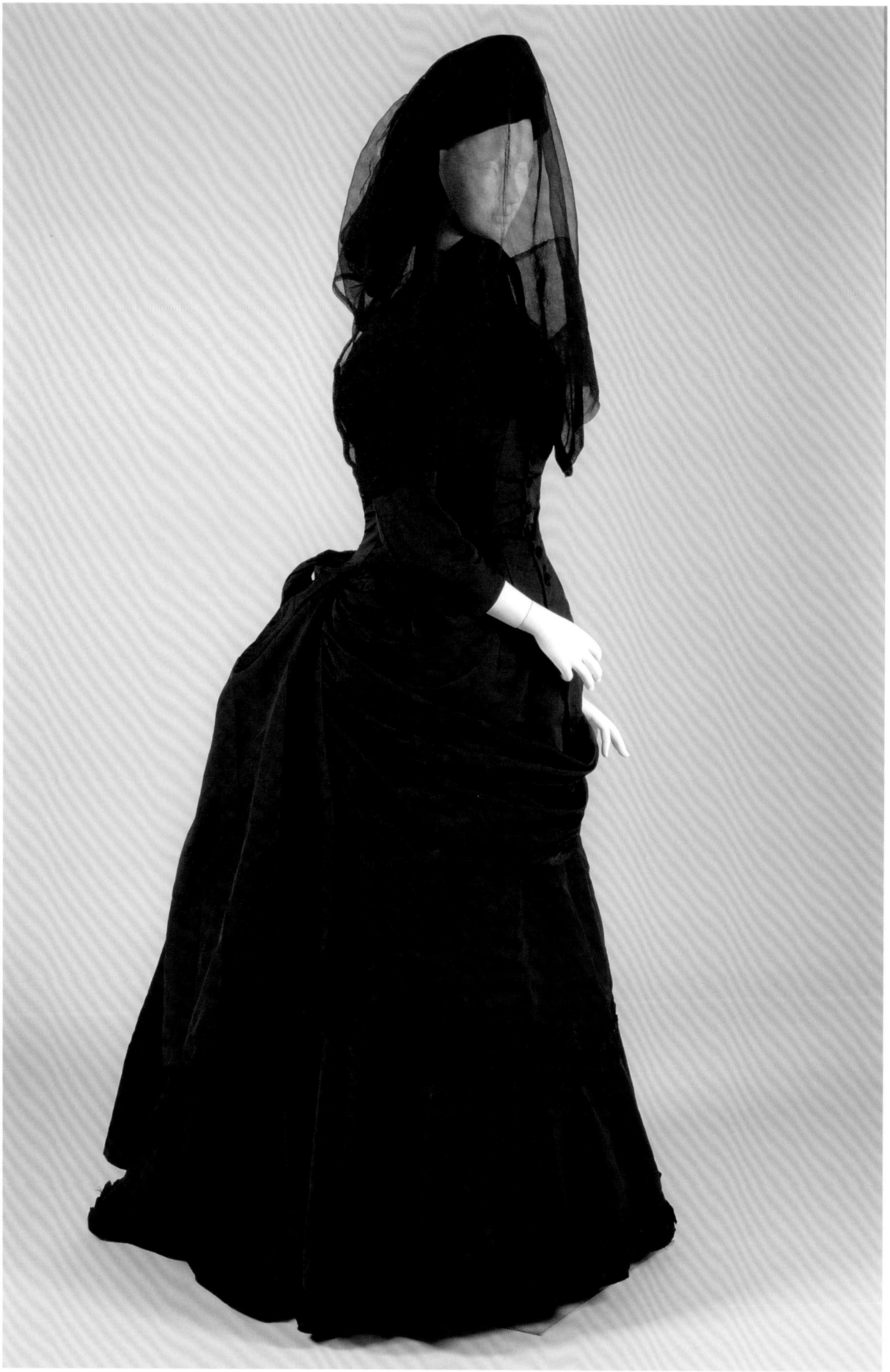

as well as the symbolism of magic and authority. Especially important, however, was the overall blackness of his clothing, which evoked a complex philosophy of diabolism, dandyism and decadence, as will be seen.

Female cinematic vampires, in contrast, have tended to wear pale, usually white, flowing dresses that negotiate between the timeless and the currently fashionable. Variants of the theme can be seen in numerous movies, including *Dracula's Daughter* (1936) and *Son of Dracula* (1942). A number of films, such as *Horror of Dracula* (1958), explicitly replicated the white neoclassical nightgown and sometimes also the pose of the woman in Fuseli's *Nightmare* – although the vampire's female victims usually wore the white of innocent virginity, while female vampires wore the white of traditional burial clothes. Eiko Ishikura's striking costumes for Francis Ford Coppola's 1992 film *Bram Stoker's Dracula* clothe the female vampires in pale gauzy dresses, accessorized with Medusa hair and glittering headdresses, while Dracula's female victims, such as Mina, wear voluptuous 1880s bustle dresses in colors such as blood red.

Throughout world history, black has been associated with night and darkness and, by extension, with death, danger, and evil. The devil has long been known

18. (facing page) Victorian mourning dress, c. 1880. Photograph: Irving Solero. Courtesy Evan Michelson.

19. (above, left) Late Victorian mourning dress, c. 1895. The Museum at the Fashion Institute of Technology, New York. Photograph: Irving Solero.

20. (above, right) Late Victorian mourning dress (detail), c. 1895. The Museum at the Fashion Institute of Technology, New York. Photograph: Irving Solero.

embrace the unhealthy and the deviant, and focus on the dark side of romanticism. Nineteenth-century culture, in general, was filled with images of death. More often than not, these were sentimental images, such as photographs of dead children, but there were also playfully transgressive images, such as the widely reproduced photograph of the young and beautiful Sarah Bernhardt playing dead in the coffin that she kept in her apartment. There were also magnificent images of royal deaths, such as the photograph of "Mad" King Ludwig of Bavaria laid out in state, after his untimely death.

The *femme fatale* was often, although not always depicted in black. Barbey d'Aurevilly's story "Happiness in Crime" from *Les Diaboliques* (1874) shows how a decadent writer interpreted black clothing. Himself a famous dandy, d'Aurevilly described a strange couple – a "haughty, effeminate" man in "a trim black frock coat" and a tall muscular woman "dressed entirely in black." The woman is explicitly compared with a caged panther in the zoo. The animal's fur is said to be velvet, the woman's dress "gleaming" satin – "but satin is stronger than velvet." "Black, supple, as powerfully muscular, as royal in bearing – as beautiful for her own species, and with a charm still more disquieting – this woman, this unknown person, was like a human panther . . . "[23]

Silent films early in the twentieth century established the image of the black-clad vamp, as played by such actresses as Theda Bara. Charles Addams first portrayed the glamorously gothic Morticia in a cartoon of 1938 in which she wears a long, tight black gown with a plunging décolletage and dangling sleeves. Asked if she had been modeled on anyone in particular, the cartoonist claimed that she was "more or less something from my own head" – "just my idea of a pretty girl"

27. (left) "The Great Sarah Bernhardt Asleep in her Coffin," c. 1882. Silver gelatin print. Courtesy Stanley B. Burns, MD, The Burns Archive.

28. (right) "'Mad' King Ludwig of Bavaria, the Drowned Swan King," 1886. Cabinet card by Frz. Werner, Munich. Courtesy Stanley B. Burns, MD, The Burns Archive.

29. (left) Theda Bara as Rosa in *Sin*, 1915. Fox Film Corporation.

30. (right) Bat belt buckle, c. 1900. Gunmetal with paste. Courtesy Collection of Mark Walsh and Leslie Chin. Photograph: Irving Solero.

31. "Countess de Castiglione as the Queen of the Night," 1863–7. Photograph by Pierre-Louis Pierson. Courtesy The Metropolitan Museum of Art, Gilman Collection. Gift of The Howard Gilman Foundation, 2005 (2005.100.405). Image © The Metropolitan Museum of Art.

— although he admitted that "there might be a little Gloria Swanson in her."[24] Morticia Addams was later joined on television by Elvira and Vampira, whose appearance helped establish the enduring image of the gothic *femme fatale*.

Gabrielle "Coco" Chanel is widely credited with having "invented" the little black dress in the 1920s, transforming its significance from mourning to elegance. This is untrue. Although the dominant nineteenth-century image of the woman in black was indeed the woman in mourning attire, black clothing was not only worn for mourning. From the princely black of the Renaissance to Sargeant's infamous portrait of *Madame X* (1886), black has often symbolized elegance. Black was ascetic, but it was also erotic. The powerful image of men in black, associated with the rise of capitalism, made it all the more striking when women adopted all-black clothing. The Amazon's man-tailored riding habit was almost invariably black. Poor women wore black, because it was practical, but rich women regarded it as

32. Emile Deroy, *Portrait of Charles Baudelaire*, 1844. Oil on canvas. Chateaux de Versailles et de Trianon, Versailles, France. Courtesy Réunion des Musées Nationaux/Art Resource, NY.

the most elegant and flattering color, and it was popular for fancy dress costumes like "The Queen of the Night".

Black clothing was also associated with the elegantly Satanic figure of the dandy. According to the literary scholar Catherine Spooner, "Dandy and Gothic hero-villain evolved in a symbiotic partnership over the course of the century."[25] It was not merely that real-life dandies were inspired by the hero-villains of Gothic novels, although this was certainly often the case. The philosophy of dandyism also resonated with the spirit of the fictional Gothic aristocrat.

The first important analysis of dandyism is a brief, elusive masterpiece written by Barbey d'Aurevilly in 1845. Ostensibly a portrait of George "Beau" Brummell as the *Ur-*dandy, the book is also a passionate argument that the dandy is far more than merely Carlyle's "Clothes-wearing Man." D'Aurevilly insists that dandyism "is not a suit of clothes walking about by itself! On the contrary, it is the particular way of wearing these clothes that constitutes Dandyism."[26] The dandy wears his clothing "like armour" with an "air of elegant indifference" and *sang-froid*.[27]

Although d'Aurevilly was a pioneer in the theorizing of dandyism, it was Charles Baudelaire, author of the banned book of poems *The Flowers of Evil*, who really established the figure of the dandy as the elegant, black-clad hero of modern life. In his youth in the 1840s, Baudelaire dressed all in black, "at every hour, in every season." He looked, a friend recalled, like "Byron dressed by Beau Brummell."[28] In other words, he combined the fascinating wickedness of the Byronic fatal man with the cool, disciplined austerity of the Regency dandy. Baudelaire was not only personally a dandy, he was also instrumental in developing the philosophy of dandyism, especially in his essay "The Painter of Modern Life" (1863). Moreover, he was not alone in his obsession with black clothes and English dandies. "English black is the shade most worn," announced the fashion magazine *Le Dandy* (1838), while *La Presse* (1859) declared that

> [The dandy is] the Black Prince of elegance, the demi-god of ennui, looking at the world with a glassy eye . . . Indifferent to the horse that he mounts, to the woman that he greets, to the man that he approaches and at whom he stares for a moment before acknowledging him, and wearing written on his forehead – in English – this insolent inscription: *What is there in common between you and me?*[29]

What is there in common between you and me? Every black-clad anti-hero is indebted to the nineteenth-century dandy for this proud claim of elite outsider status. The image of the dandy as a cold and blasé foreign gentleman with a basilisk stare and an ambiguous sexual orientation gradually merged with the popular image of the vampire. Just as the devil is the prince of darkness, the dandy is the black prince of elegance – and the paradigm of the gothic man is a dandy vampire aristocrat. Who then is the gothic woman? Can she be a dandy, too?

Baudelaire insisted in no uncertain terms that "Woman is the opposite of the dandy," because she is "natural."[30] Yet elsewhere he implied that, just as the dandy was a modern self-creation, so also did women turn themselves into works of art through their use of modern fashion and cosmetics. In contemporary terms, it would be said that dandyism for both sexes is performative. Indeed, in an extraordinary passage, d'Aurevilly describes dandies in the following terms: "These Stoics of the boudoir drink their own blood under their mask and remain masked. For Dandies, as for women, to *seem* is to *be*."[31]

Consider that last statement again: "*Paraître, c'est être, pour les Dandys comme pour les femmes.*" (*To seem* [or *to appear*] is *to be*, for Dandys as for women.) Although dandyism has traditionally been regarded as an essentially masculine phenomenon, in recent years the concept of the female dandy has intrigued theorists. In particular, attention has turned to Gabrielle "Coco" Chanel, who introduced female dandyism into high fashion, having first explored its potential in her complicated personal life. As Chanel told Salvador Dalí, speaking of herself in the third person, "She took the English masculine and made it feminine. All her life, all she did was change men's clothing into women's."[32] As Barbara Vinken has put it in her book *Fashion Zeitgeist* (2004). "One easily recognizes that the godfather of this new femininity under the sign of the masculine was not

33. Ensemble by Burberry Prorsum, necklaces by Malcolm Guerre, styling by Nicola Formichetti, *Dazed and Confused,* August 2007. Photograph courtesy Mariano Vivanco.

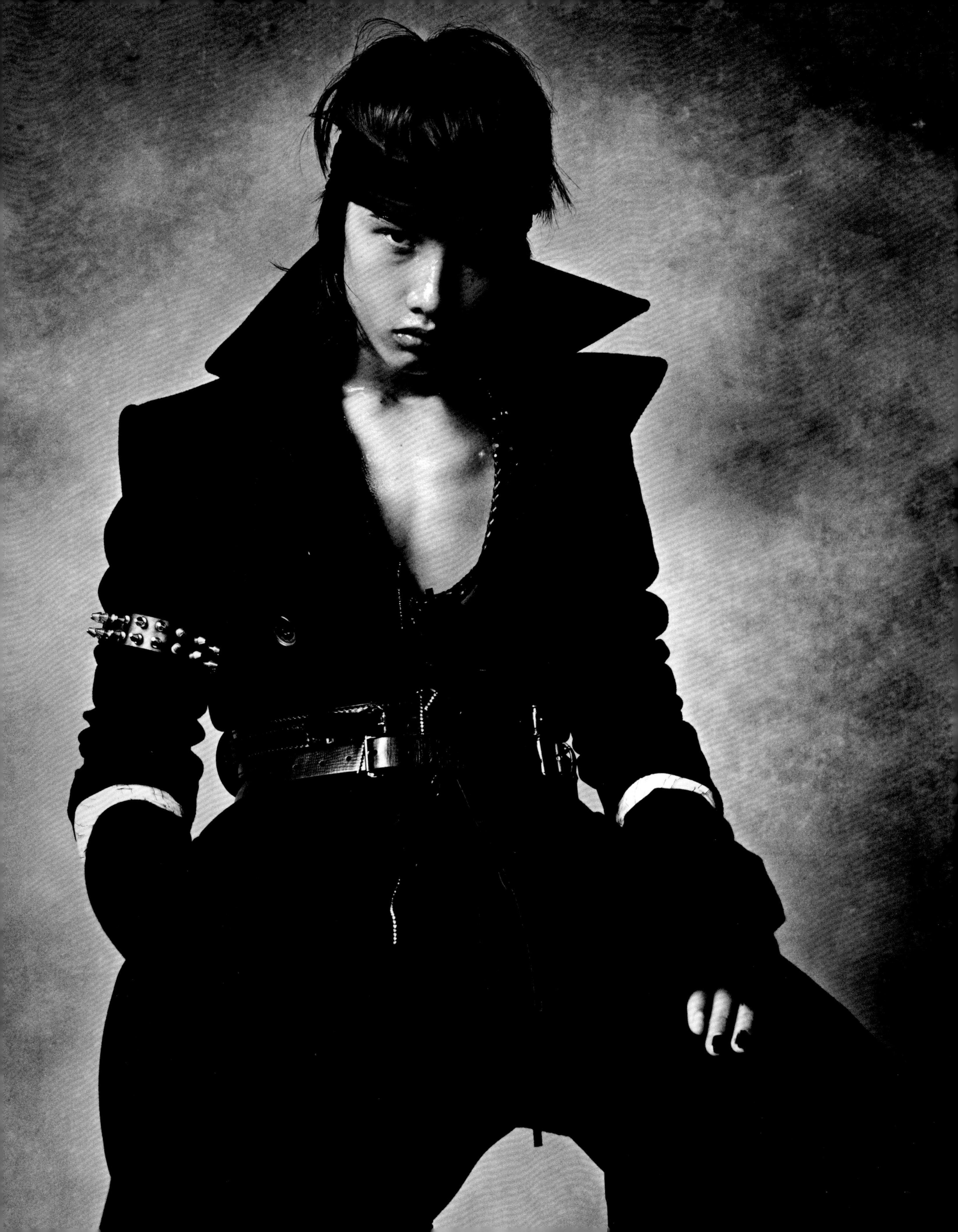

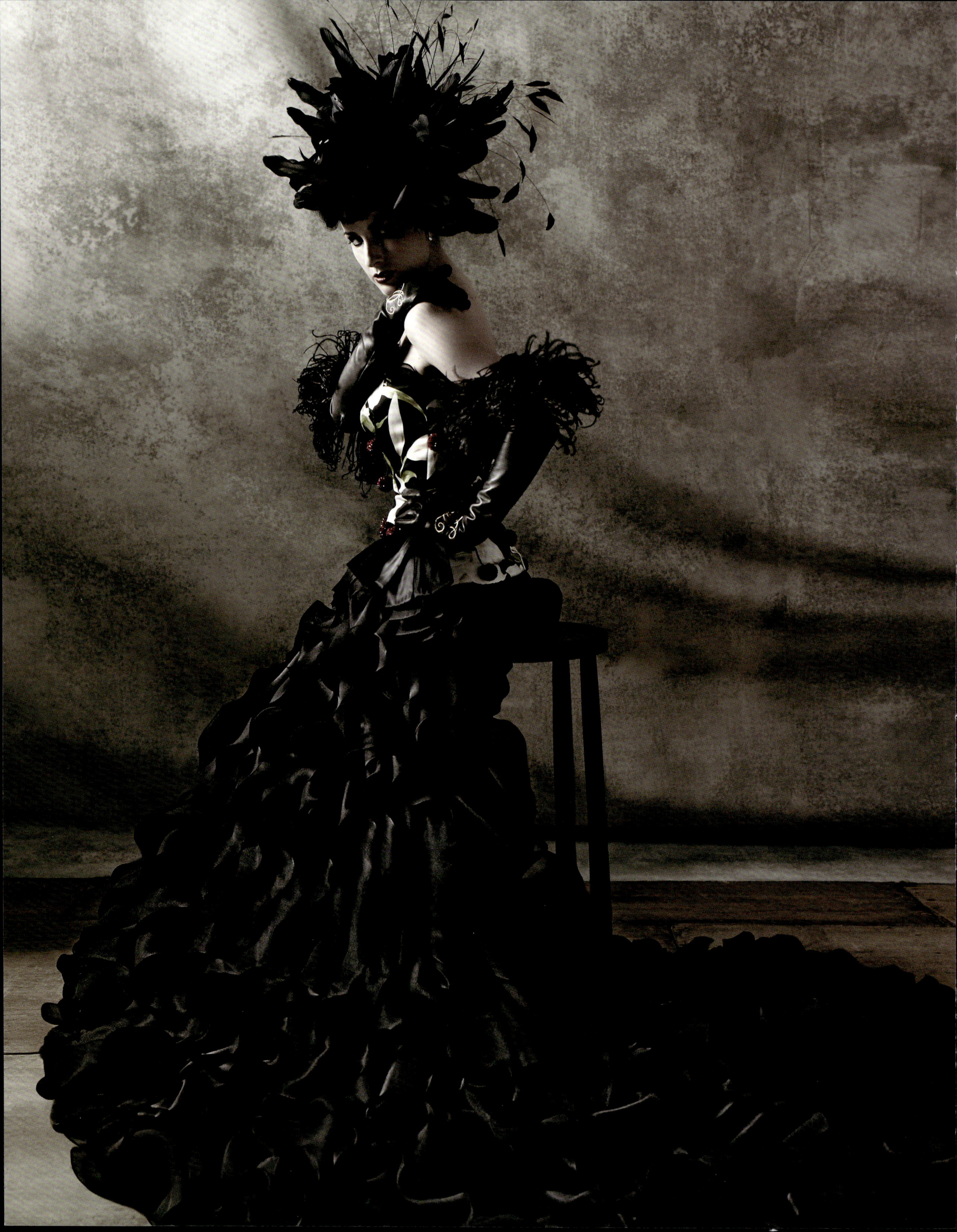

the sexually unmarked bourgeois man, but the dandy, celebrated by Baudelaire." It was not merely that "Chanel paid him a lasting homage in . . . her spare and perfect 'little black dress'." More significant was the manner in which Chanel's fashion was worn, for "the carefully cultivated appearance of not having invested any thought into the clothes that one wears – all this belongs to the credo of the perfect dandy."[33] Indeed, Vinken goes on to argue that contemporary fashion essentially offers women only two choices: to dress as a dandy *à la Chanel*, or as a transvestite, *à la Dior*. But "whether as a dandy or as a dream woman, it is not possible to dress oneself 'naturally'." In other words, "Fashion represents . . . the impossibility . . . of not wearing a mask."[34]

34. Dita von Teese in a gown by Dress Camp, *Vogue* Nippon, November 2006. Creative Consultant: Gene Krell. Photograph: YASUNARI KIKUMA. Courtesy YASUNARI KIKUMA, *Vogue* Nippon, and www.dita.net.

subculture and style

> "Gothic. Kinky. Tattooed. Vampire . . . This is sex for you." *Blue Blood*, c. 1995

Subcultures are usually defined as groups of young people who are in opposition to the dominant culture. Typically, subcultures are seen in terms of a succession of distinctive styles (hippy, punk, goth, and so on) that are performed as a type of symbolic resistance to the oppressive mainstream society. The perceived authenticity of subcultural style has led to its being mythologized as a direct expression of individual creativity and a badge of subcultural identity. By contrast, fashion is often demonized as the product of an industry based on conformity, superficiality, and stylistic changes that are meaningless except in terms of the profit motive. What was once innovative, even "subversive" within a subculture becomes merely "trendy" once it is assimilated into the commercial world of fashion. Yet the relationship between subcultural style and mainstream fashion is much more complicated than the stereotype of co-optation would imply.

Reacting against the love and peace of the hippies, the punks created a musically angry and profane style of music in the mid-1970s. Sartorially, punk was characterized by a look of "kinky nihilism" featuring sinister black leather, fetishistic rubber and PVC garments, dog collars, bondage trousers, and obscene T-shirts, as well as aggressively spiky hairstyles and body-piercing. A style in revolt, punk was also a deliberately revolting style. Yet the taboo-breaking punk look quickly influenced the fashion mainstream. The fashion designer most closely associated with the punks was Vivienne Westwood, herself a punk, whose London shop Sex catered to both punks and hard-core fetishists, and whose boyfriend Malcolm McLaren was the manager of the punk rock band the Sex Pistols. As the shock of punk began to diminish, and the "hard punk" look became increasingly stereotyped, other subcultural styles, such as goth, emerged from the punk matrix.

Meanwhile, in Paris, the fashion designer Karl Lagerfeld held his famous Soirée Moratoire Noire party on October 24, 1977, after the Chloé fashion show. The

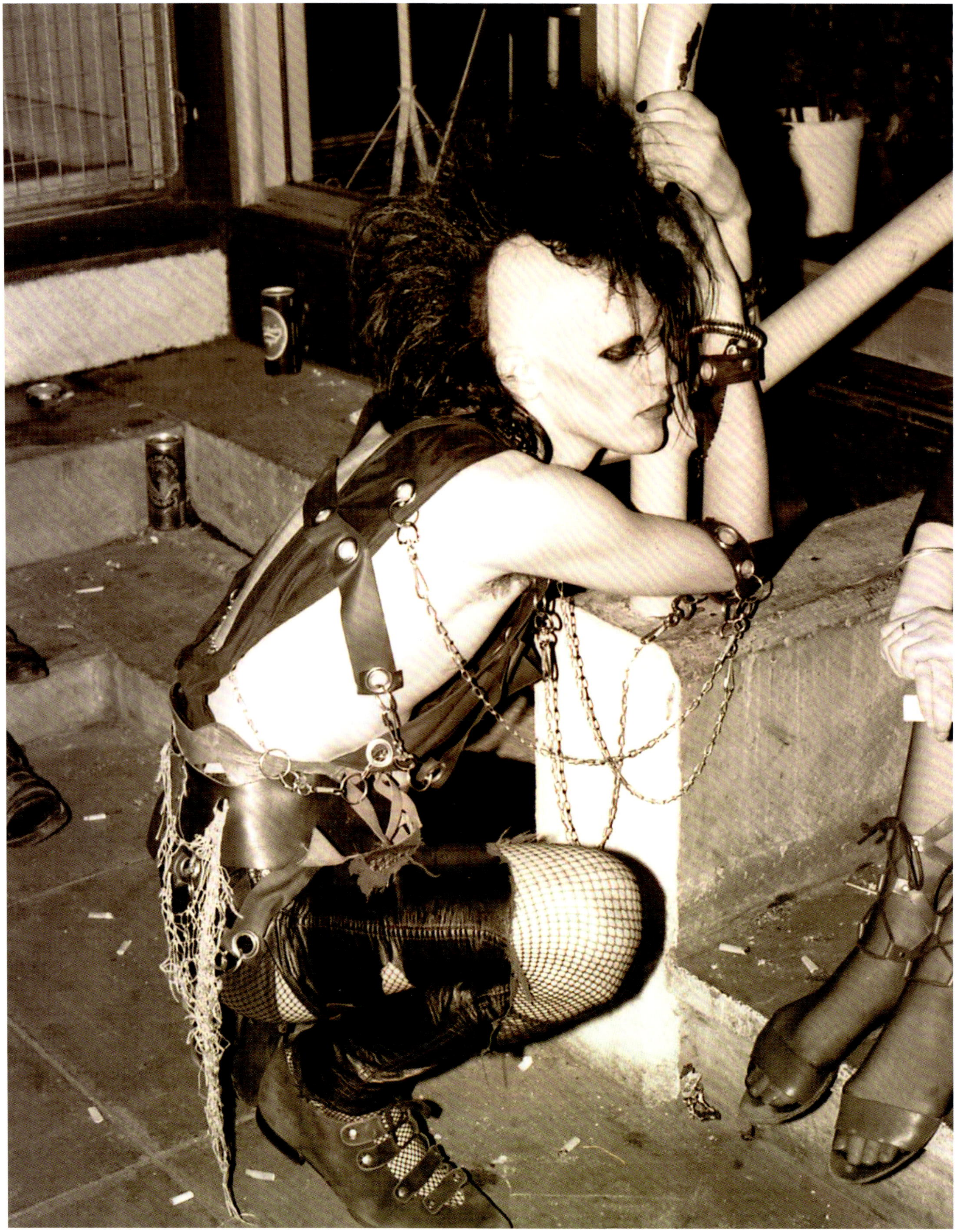

invitation read: "Moratoire Noire – tenue tragique exigée absolument noire" (Black Moratorium – totally black tragic dress required). The party was arranged by Lagerfeld's friend Jacques de Bascher and was intended as a transgressive saturnalia, complete with S&M performances and thousands of people dressed all in black. As Lagerfeld said, "We have had enough of those parties full of blond women with year-round tans."[35]

35. Jonny Slut at the Batcave, London, August 10, 1983. Photograph courtesy Mick Mercer.

The party-goers, however, were not wearing the kind of worldly, elegant, and alluring black that fashion magazines had promoted since the 1950s. The phenomenon known as "terrorist chic" had moved from the periphery, where it was associated particularly with the gay leatherman style, to the center of fashion. The French designer Claude Montana attended Lagerfeld's party dressed entirely in black leather, evoking both the sadomasochistic allure of leathersex and the "fascist chic" of black SS uniforms. Montana could simultaneously embrace the subcultural look of S&M black leather and also set trends within the world of high fashion, just as Westwood could be both a punk and a fashion designer. Indeed, so ubiquitous was the look that even the Montgomery Ward department store in America featured S&M-style black leather fashion in the 1970s. Fashion styling and advertising also increasingly emphasized themes of dominance and submission, as photographers such as Guy Bourdin and Helmut Newton were accused of turning fashion photography into pornography.[36] The boundaries between fashion and subculture were extremely porous, with many individuals navigating back and forth.

Boundaries between subcultures were even more fluid. When the goth subculture developed in the late 1970s, "on the heels of punk's infamous rebellion," fans of the emerging style of music were sometimes referred to as "gothic punks."[37] Like punk, goth embraced both a style of music and a style of dress, although people who look like goths do not necessarily listen to the music, and vice-versa. In both musical and sartorial terms, goth developed out of punk some time between 1979 and 1981. The first generation of British post-punk bands that have been labeled "gothic" include Bauhaus, Siouxsie & the Banshees, The Cure, UK Decay, and Sisters of Mercy.

Bauhaus's debut single, "Bela Lugosi's Dead" (1979), is sometimes regarded as the true beginning of gothic rock, and the band was featured playing it in the stylish vampire movie, *The Hunger* (1983), starring David Bowie. From 1997 through 1999, the song was also used to introduce the recurring sketch "Goth Talk" on the television program *Saturday Night Live*, which relentlessly mocked the pretensions of teenaged goths. Goth style, however, developed only gradually. The members of Bauhaus, for example, initially wore ordinary jeans and T-shirts, and only later adopted all-black clothing and striking make-up.

By 1982, the goth subculture was in full bloom. New bands continued to emerge, including Southern Death Cult, Sex Gang Children, and Alien Sex Fiend. Other seminal goth bands include Fields of the Nephilim, Ministry, Dead Can Dance, the Mission, the Wake, and Mephisto Waltz. Meanwhile, a "deathrock" scene had developed in Los Angeles with bands such as Christian Death and clubs like Helter Skelter. Deathrock could be described as the form that goth first

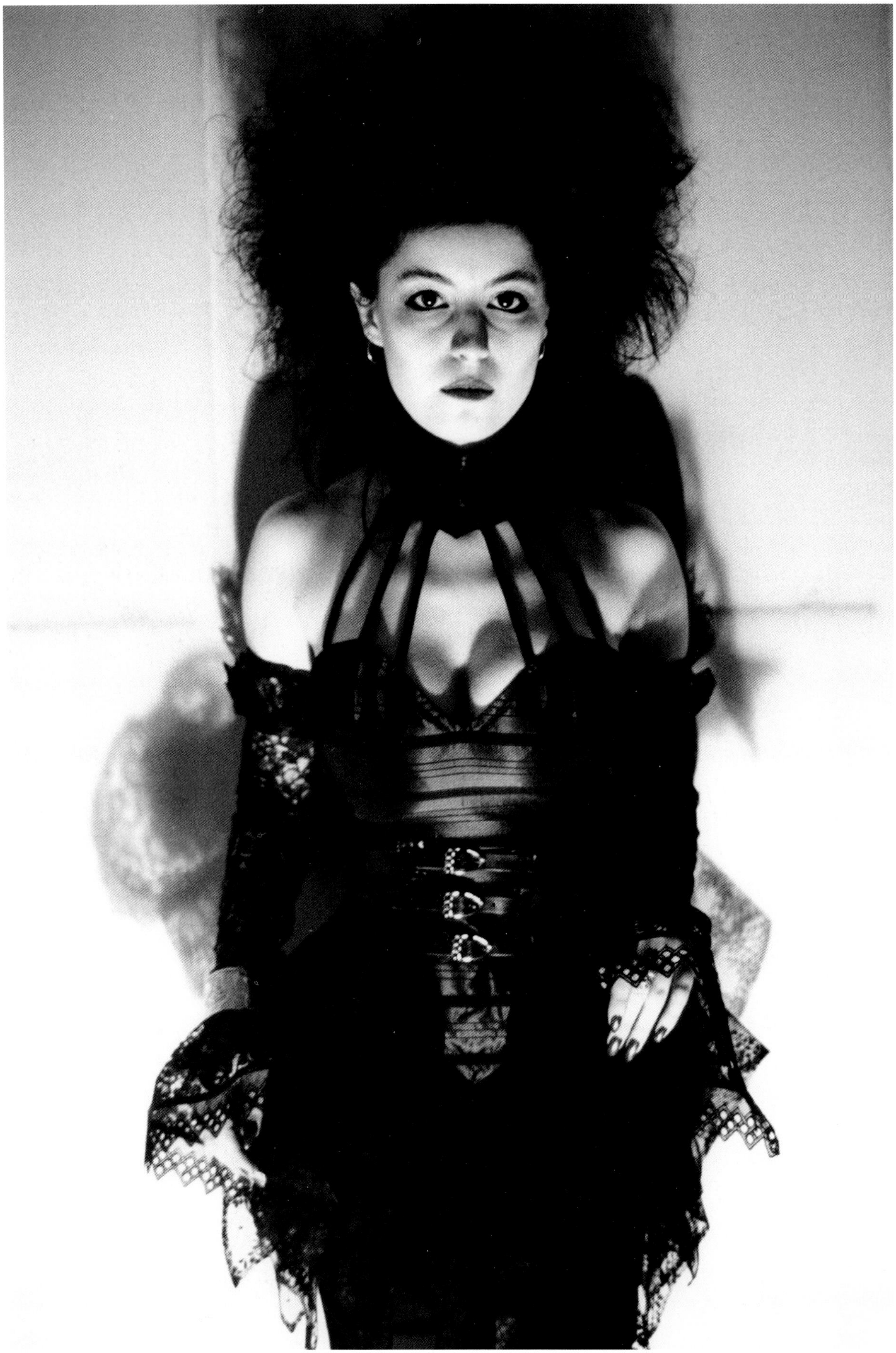

took in America, as the New York punk style moved west and merged with a Southern California sense of suburban angst (Jennifer Park provides a much more detailed analysis of post-punk music later in this book).

"The Goths continued the Punks' interest in fetishism and translated it into a more dressy, extravagant style," recalls Ted Polhemus, an American based in London who has spent years studying style tribes.[38] Like the punks, goths incorporated elements of "perv" or fetish fashions, but like the New Romantics, another English style tribe, they also gravitated toward extravagant, vaguely historical styles. The fashions of Victorian England were influential, especially among goths living in England, but goth style was a deliberate pastiche: Victorian corsets and shiny black PVC, mourning veils, and trashy fishnet stockings. Leather was popular but so were "feminine" materials such as velvet and lace. Footwear ranged from punkish Doc Martens to witchy, Victorian-style lace-up boots. Whereas classic punk style emphasized masculinity, goths increasingly favored an androgynous style, including make-up and skirts for men.

When the famous club the Batcave opened in London, its motto was "Blasphemy, Lechery, and Blood."[39] Punk's nihilism and fetishism, David Bowie's vision of glam rock, and a darker, horror-influenced style all merged. The goth "death look" was created with pale white foundation, black eyeliner, black nail polish, and dark black-red lipstick. Whereas punks favored lurid, brightly colored mohawks,

36. (facing page) The club organizer Anna Goodman wearing clothes from the Kensington Market gothic shop Symphony of Shadows, London, 1982. Photograph courtesy Ted Polhemus.

37. (above) Goth woman at the opening night of the Batcave, London, 1981. Photograph courtesy Ted Polhemus.

goths tended to dye their hair black or white-blond. Vampires were a source of inspiration, contributing to the popular "I just crawled out of the grave" look. Above all, goth clothing was entirely or predominantly black.

Since goth style is easy to stereotype, and since it has evolved over time, it is important to hear directly from people who identify themselves as goths or who remember being goths when they were younger. Fortunately, goths tend to be extremely articulate.

Growing up in southern California, Patricia Morrison recognized early that the "blonde, blue-eyed look wasn't me" and moved to London in 1983. A member of the post-punk band, the Gun Club ("the term 'goth' hadn't been coined"), she joined and then left the Sisters of Mercy. Known for her dark glamour, she later married another icon of goth style, Dave Vanian, the lead singer of the post-punk band the Damned. Vanian was a former grave digger who sometimes dressed up as a vampire on stage, which influenced other performers and fans. Morrison recalls that, while Vanian liked Hammer horror films, she was definitely "*not* trying to have any horror image," although she admitted that "the vampire component was there" and her make-up became increasingly "dramatic." Ultimately, though, she insists that "Unlike some people today who are very horror and trying to shock, we were trying to look good."[40]

Like punk, goth was initially a do-it-yourself style. Individuals often made their own clothing or modified existing garments. "There were small shops in London and New York [in the 1980s] that sold gothy things," recalls Evan Michelson, but "none of us wore designer clothes. There was a lot of artistic cutting and shredding, ripped fishnets, and things being held together by safety pins." Evan, who formed a "feminist industrial goth band" in the 1980s called Killer Weasel, remembers that goth boys "wore dresses," which was "more transgressive – the police would stop them." She and her boyfriend (who had long black hair and looked, in her words, "pale and completely androgynous") boiled animal bones and strung them to wear as necklaces, along with little "voodoo" bags, full of toenails and hair.

38. (left) Bat buckle shoes, designed by Black of England, 1990. Photograph: Irving Solero. Courtesy Pandora Harrison.

39. (right) The jewelry designer Morticia, in her own designs of skeleton earrings and chicken-bone necklace, at her shop in Camden Market, London, early 1980s. Photograph courtesy Ted Polhemus.

40. (left) Patricia Morrison performing with Gun Club at the Lyceum, London, December 4, 1983. Photograph courtesy Mick Mercer.

41. (right) David Vanian performing with the Damned at the Hammersmith Palais, London, September 9, 1983. Photograph courtesy Mick Mercer.

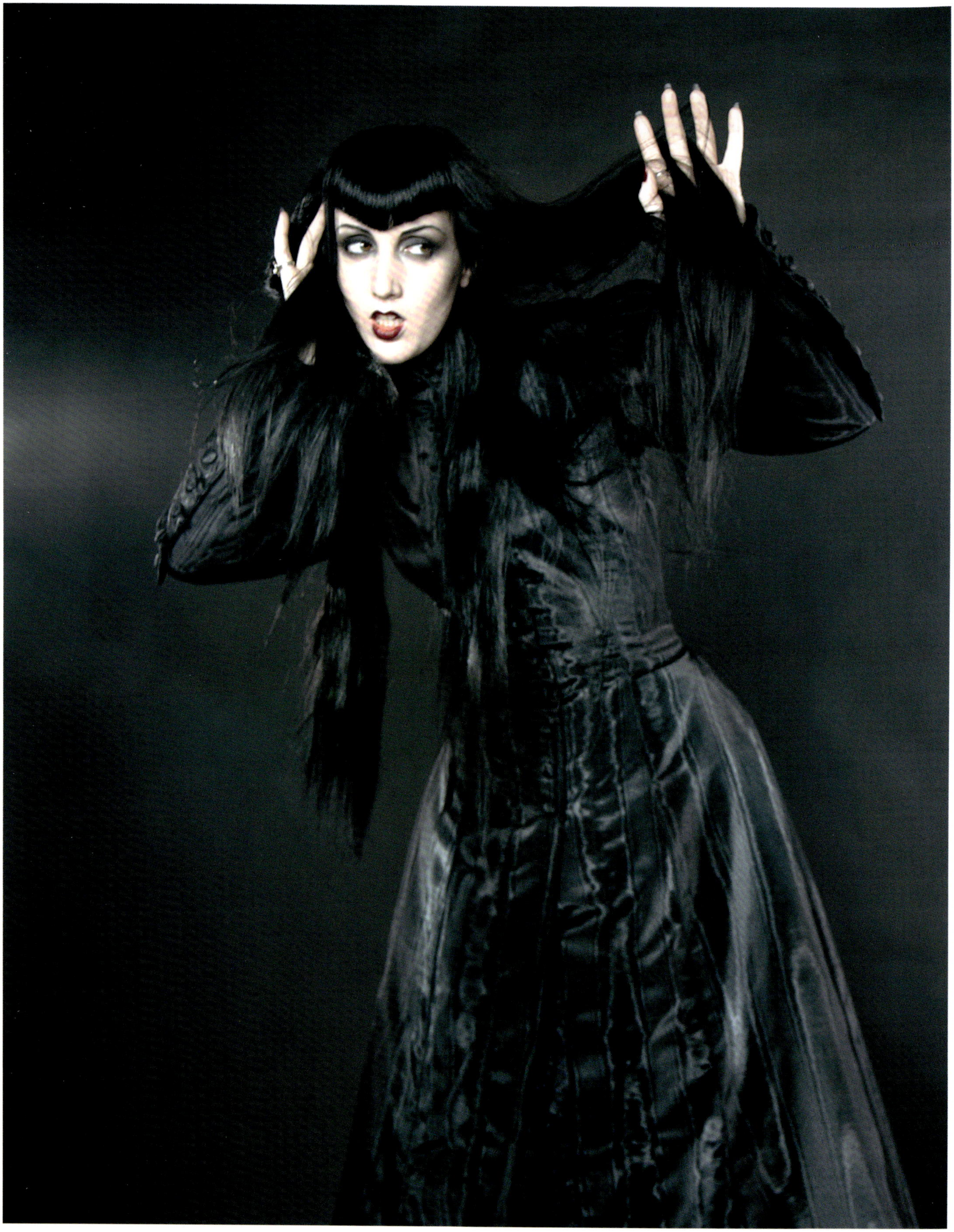

wear gas masks or (in what appears to be a kind of medical fetish) shiny PVC doctors' masks. "The look is quite androgynous and similar for both men and women." Meanwhile, the industrial goth look has incorporated exotic camouflage prints, such as arctic camo. Yet another popular style is the gothabilly look, which combines black 1950s vintage with fetish elements such as corsets or merry widows and shredded thigh-highs. "Today a Goth might dress with a few Cyber elements or a few Industrial elements," explains Julia. "Events usually dictate the type of dress one will don." For example, if you expect to hear a particular kind of music at a club or concert, you would dress accordingly. Yet "no matter what you wear, you're still accepted by the subculture. Straight, gay, male, female, punk, industrial, even metal, one is always welcomed".[55]

56. (facing page) Kambriel, "Isabella Coatdress," worn by Wednesday Mourning. Courtesy Kambriel. Photograph: Nadya Lev.

57. (above) Cyber goth look by Plastik Wrap, worn by Hilary Gillespie. Courtesy Plastik Wrap. Photograph: Jeff Turner.

58. (following page) Cyber-goth photo by Eric Charles. © 2008 Eric Charles, All Rights Reserved.

59. (page 53) John Galliano for Christian Dior, Haute Couture Fall/Winter 1999. Courtesy Roxanne Lowit Photographs.

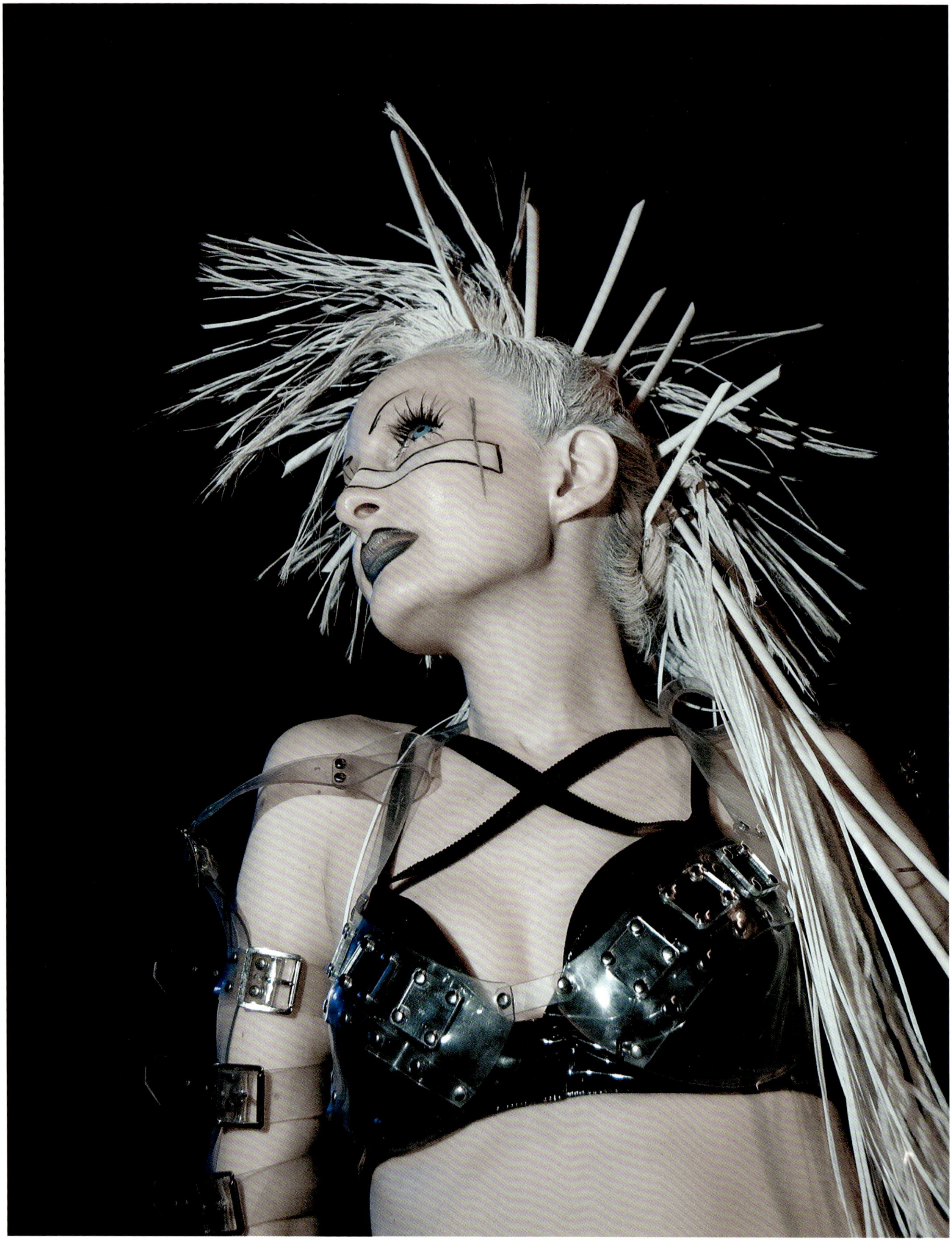

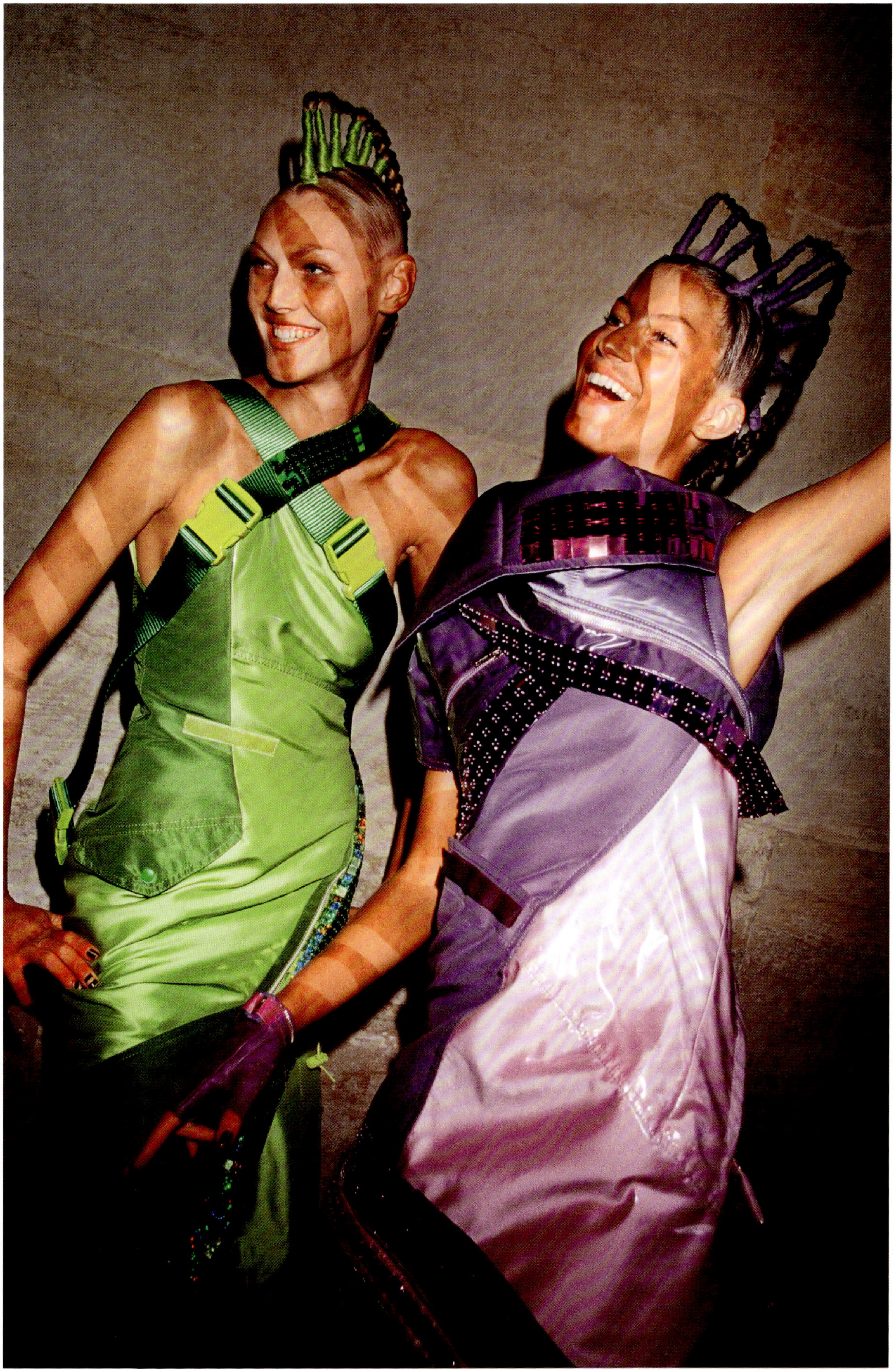

Among the many goth clothing businesses on the web, several stand out. One of the best classic sites, formerly known as Atrocities, now goes under the name of the designer, Kambriel, creator of "Designs for Femmes Fatales & Decadent Gentlemen." After the relatively aggressive punk scene, she was drawn to the "nocturnal dream-world" of the emerging goth scene. Over time, however, the "poetic," "long and flowing" clothes of the original goths seemed to disappear, and "even the more underground styles" became "harsher" and "more fetishistic." Surrounded by form-fitting PVC garments, she found herself "longing for something softer" and "eerily beautiful." Kambriel designed her first "Gothick" collection in 1994. "For me, gothic is all about finding beauty in the shadows," says Kambriel. "It's about viewing the world through a Tim Burton-esque lens, in which dark humour meets intelligent irony." She recalls that "When I was very young, I strongly wished to live in another time since I felt so out of place in the current world." However, she gradually realized that she wanted "to romanticize the past into a place of pure dreams, conjuring up images of a grand masked ball, in which elegant ladies and gentlemen from various cultures and eras are gathered together for an evening of enchantment and mystery."[56] Kambriel's work exemplifies the romantic goth aesthetic, which is characterized by soft, fluid fabrics and historically inspired styles. By contrast, Plastik Wrap is a cyber-goth fashion company. The designers, Adriana Fulop and Ryan Webb, create body-conscious futuristic fashion with brightly-colored accents, which is inspired by contemporary music.

The Gothic Lolita style in Japan is another phenomenon entirely. American and European goths are quick to point out that Japanese Gothic Lolitas "do not listen to our music" and are not goths, at least in the sense that this is usually understood (although there is a separate, small goth subculture in Japan). Lolitas agree that they are not goths; they usually listen to visual-kei, a pop rock style in which the musicians wear elaborate costumes. The three black-clad members of the band Moi dix Mois, for example, have been described as "looking like a cross between The Cure, Kiss, and The Sisters of Mercy."[57] The leader of the group, Mana, was formerly the guitarist in the seminal visual-kei band Malice Mizer, which was founded in 1992. Mana is often given credit for starting the Elegant Gothic Lolita style and its corollary the Elegant Gothic Aristocrat style in 1999, when he established a fashion brand Moi-même-Moitié. Japanese popular culture has long been known for its inventive styles, and there already existed a Lolita style, but as Mana told the British anthropologist Philomena Keet, "I added a dark element to the cuteness of Lolita."[58] If the original Lolita style was characterized by girlish frills and Alice-in-Wonderland puffy skirts, Mana added gothic motifs, such as crosses, and, of course, black.

A typical Elegant Gothic Lolita look might feature a black Victorian-style dress, usually knee-length, ruffled and worn with a crinoline, together with myriad accessories, such as a parasol, bonnet, and Mary-Jane-style platform shoes. The Elegant Gothic Aristocrat might wear a black Victorian-style coat and top hat, as well as black nail polish and jewelry. Whereas western goths are very much into a DIY aesthetic, the Japanese seem to be highly focused on brands. In addition to

60. (facing page) Trevor Brown, "Grave Robber," *Gothic&LolitaBible*, Spring 2007. Courtesy Trevor Brown.

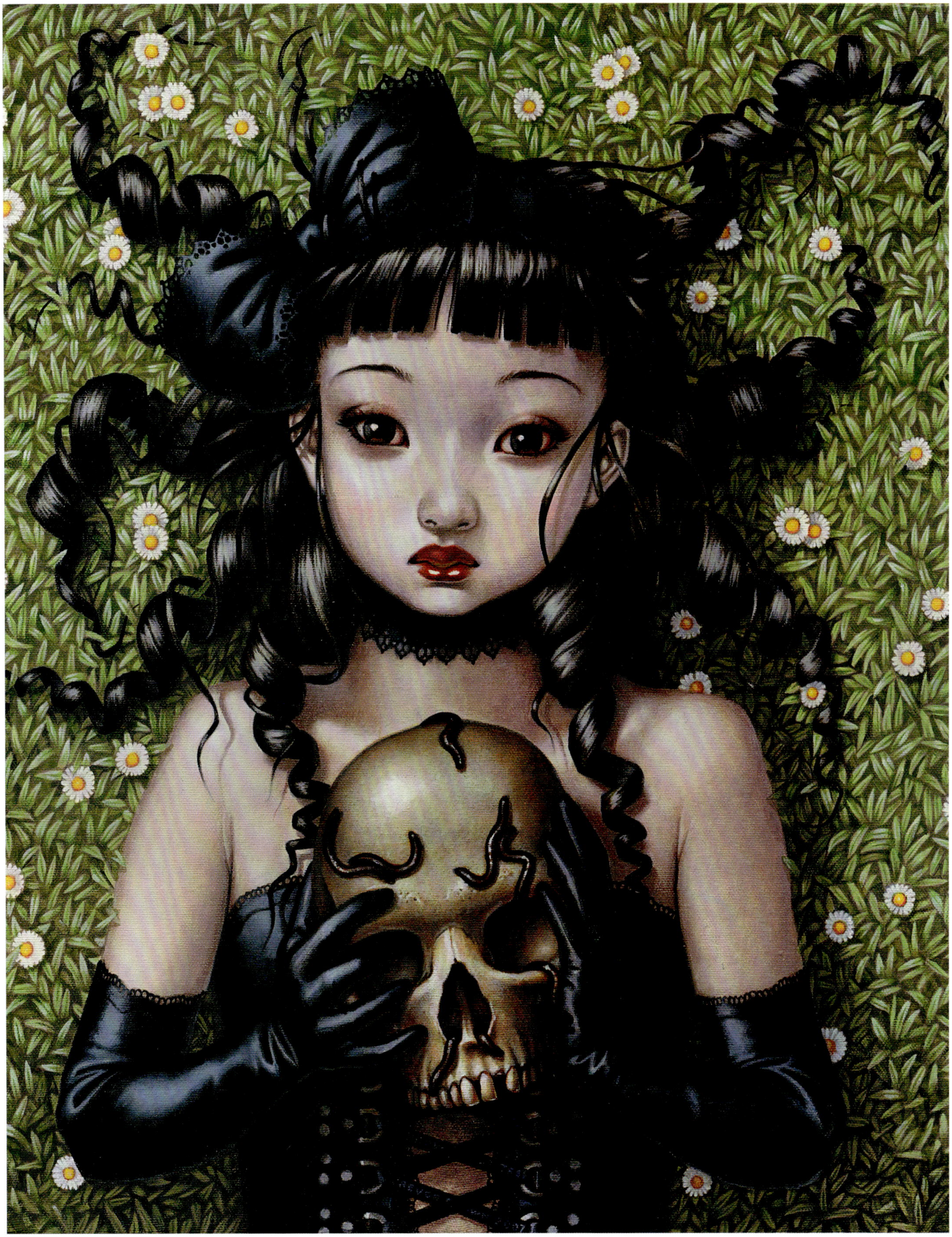

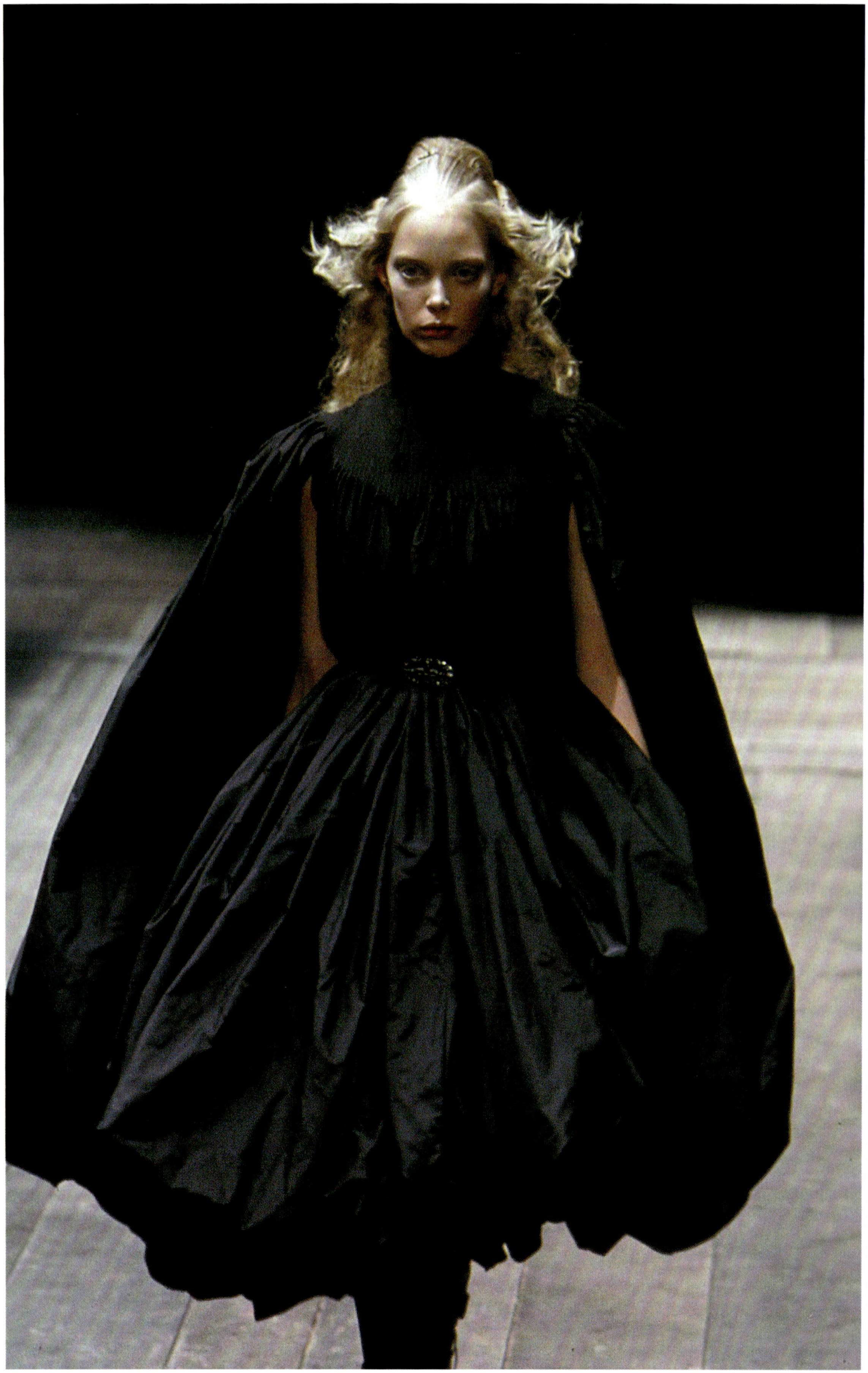

63. (facing page) Alexander McQueen Fall/Winter 2006/7. Photograph courtesy The Fashion Group Foundation.

64. (left) Jean Paul Gaultier Fall/Winter 2006/7. Photograph courtesy The Fashion Group Foundation.

black, retro-style fashions by Alexander McQueen, Jean-Paul Gaultier, and Yohji Yamamoto (somehow one is not surprised to learn that one of McQueen's ancestors was executed as a witch in Salem, Massachusetts). The great preponderance of advertising and editorial photography, however, was devoted to Japanese labels, including Angelic Pretty; Atelier-Pierrot; Baby, the Stars Shine Bright; Black Peace Now; Blood; Excentrique; Gothic & Lolita; Innocent World; Juliette et Justine; Mille Fleurs & Mille Noirs; Moi-même-Moité; Schwarze Witwe (German for "Black Widow"); Stigmata; and Victorian Maiden. There are many street photographs and some original art works.

65. (left) Masayuki Yoshinaga's portrait of Kari (left) and Seijin. Reproduced from *Gothic & Lolita*, published by Phaidon Press Limited © 2007 Phaidon Press Limited, www.phaidon.com. Courtesy Masayuki Yoshinaga.

66. (facing page) Masayuki Yoshinaga's portrait of Harold (left) and Eco. Reproduced from *Gothic & Lolita*, published by Phaidon Press Limited © 2007 Phaidon Press Limited, www.phaidon.com. Courtesy Masayuki Yoshinaga.

Japanese Gothic Lolita style has attracted considerable attention in the west and appears to be influencing some western goths. (Retroscope Fashions, for example, is a family-run internet company specializing in Japanese-style Elegant Gothic Lolita clothing and accessories for an American market.) Popular culture in general in Japan is exerting ever more influence across a variety of fields, from the popularity of *anime* to the success of Louis Vuitton's collaborations with the Japanese artist Murakami. The similarities between Trevor Brown's "Black Angel" (published in the *Gothic & Lolita Bible*) and Ruben Toledo's "Midnight Angel" (published in *Vogue Nippon*) indicate that the lines between subcultural style and high fashion have become increasingly blurred and not through any simple process of imitation.

67. (following page) "Midnight Angel," *Vogue Nippon*, November 2006. Illustration by Ruben Toledo, creative consultant Gene Krell. Courtesy Ruben Toledo and *Vogue Nippon*.

68. (page 63) Trevor Brown, "Black Angel," *Gothic&LolitaBible*, Spring 2007. Courtesy Trevor Brown.

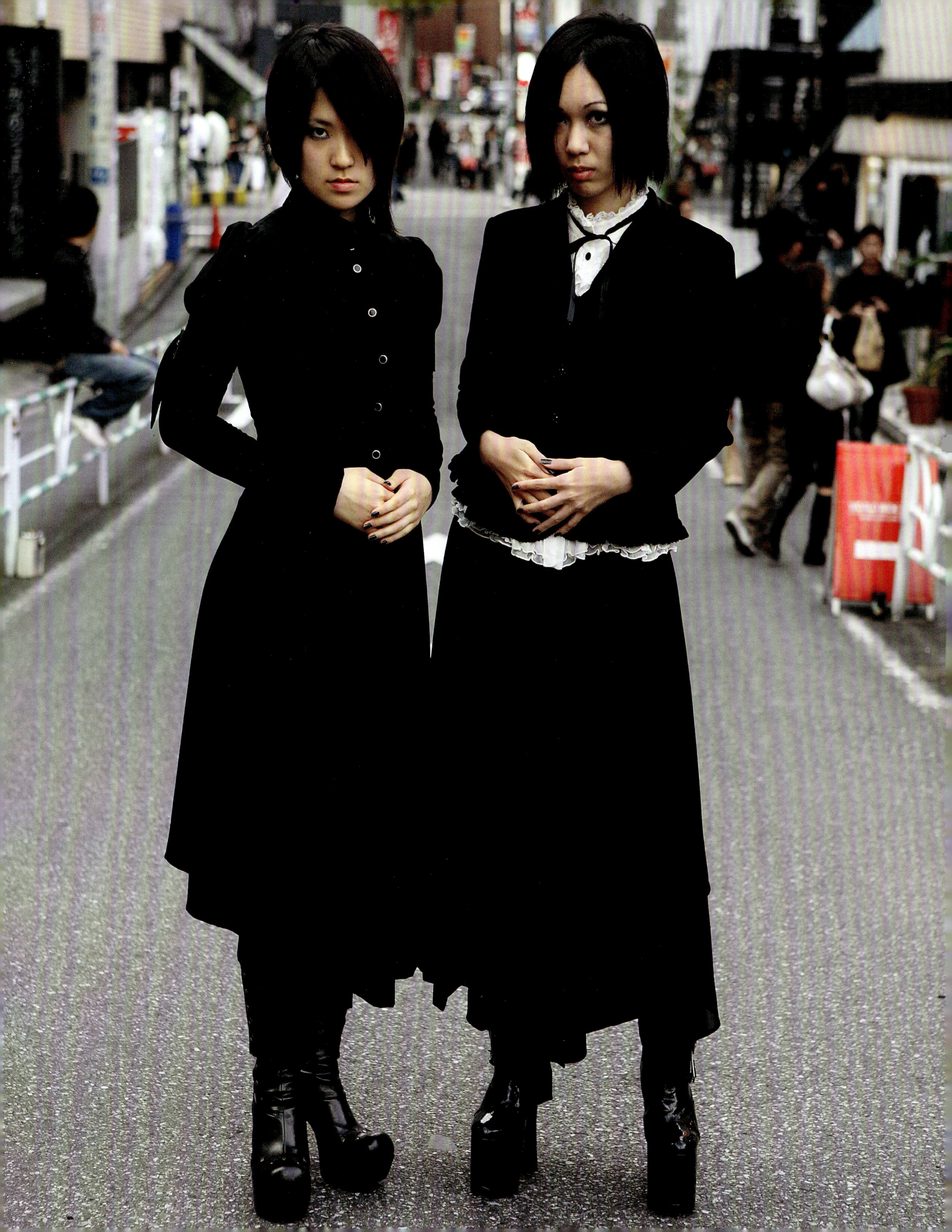

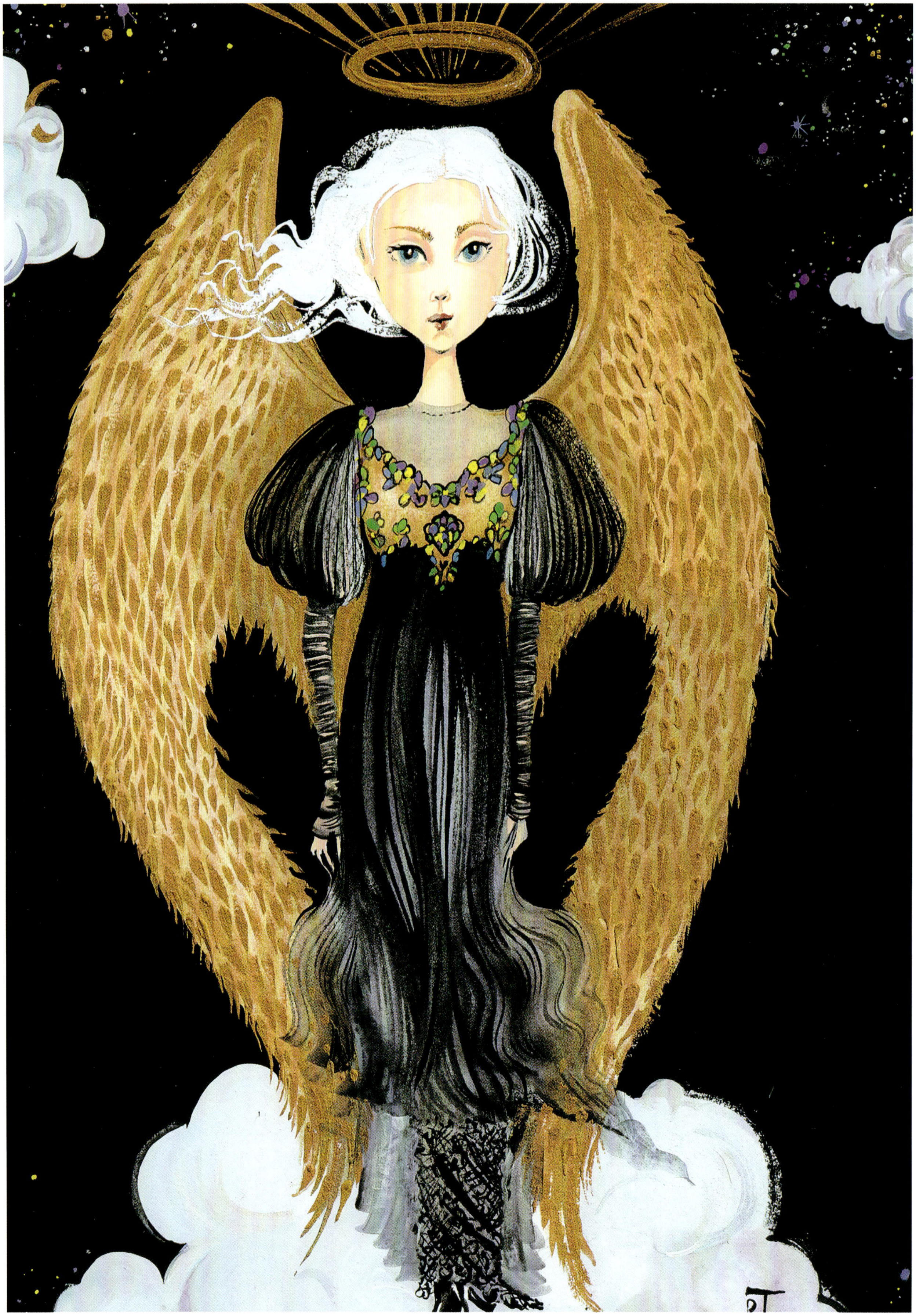

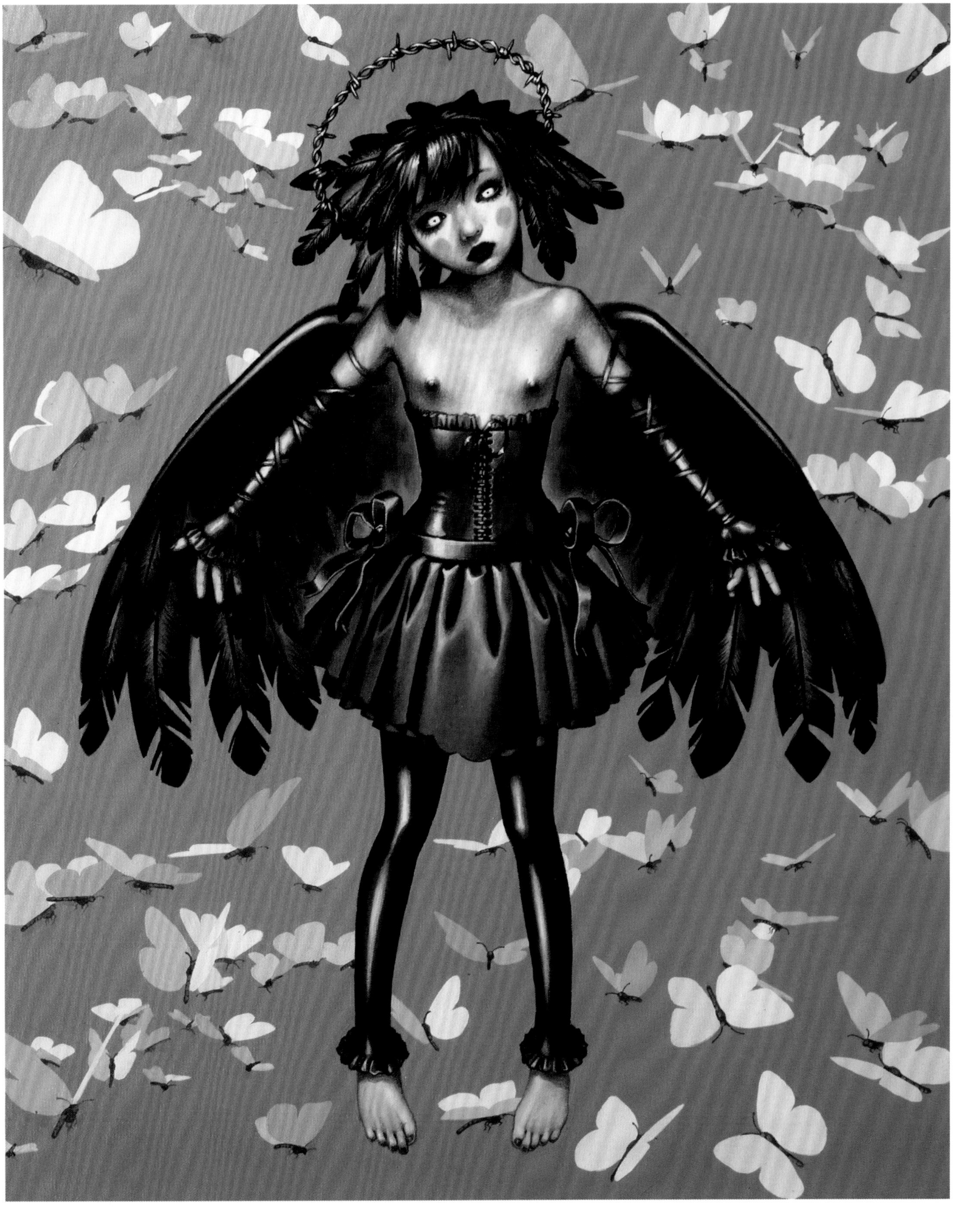

70. Elsa Schiaparelli, Skeleton Dress, 1938. Victoria and Albert Museum, London. © V&A Images.

to position themselves as artists who created unique works that aspired to a kind of ideal of beauty. This was certainly true of modernist designers, such as Chanel and Schiaparelli, different as they were in many other ways. Then, in the later part of the twentieth century, fashion reached a new stage, spectacularly marked by the 1981 Paris collections of Comme des Garçons (led by Rei Kawakubo) and Yohji Yamamoto. Their radical collections were overwhelmingly black or dark indigo blue in color, over-sized, asymmetrical, and apparently "damaged." Western journalists were horrified by what they perceived as a fashionable allegory of mortality, decadence, and mourning. Yet far from signifying death, these collections helped break the hold that death had on fashion. This, at least, is the intriguing hypothesis proposed by the German scholar Barbara Vinken. Traditionally, "fashion tried to deny death," Vinken argued, "but now it teaches us to live beautifully with death. Through fashion, one tries on one's own mortality, [revealing] the irreducible individuality of each person in the face of death." In a difficult but fascinating lecture, "Fashion, Art of Dying, Art of Living,"

71. (facing page) Alexander McQueen; headpiece by Philip Treacy. *Dante* Fall/Winter 1996–7. Courtesy Roxanne Lowit Photographs.

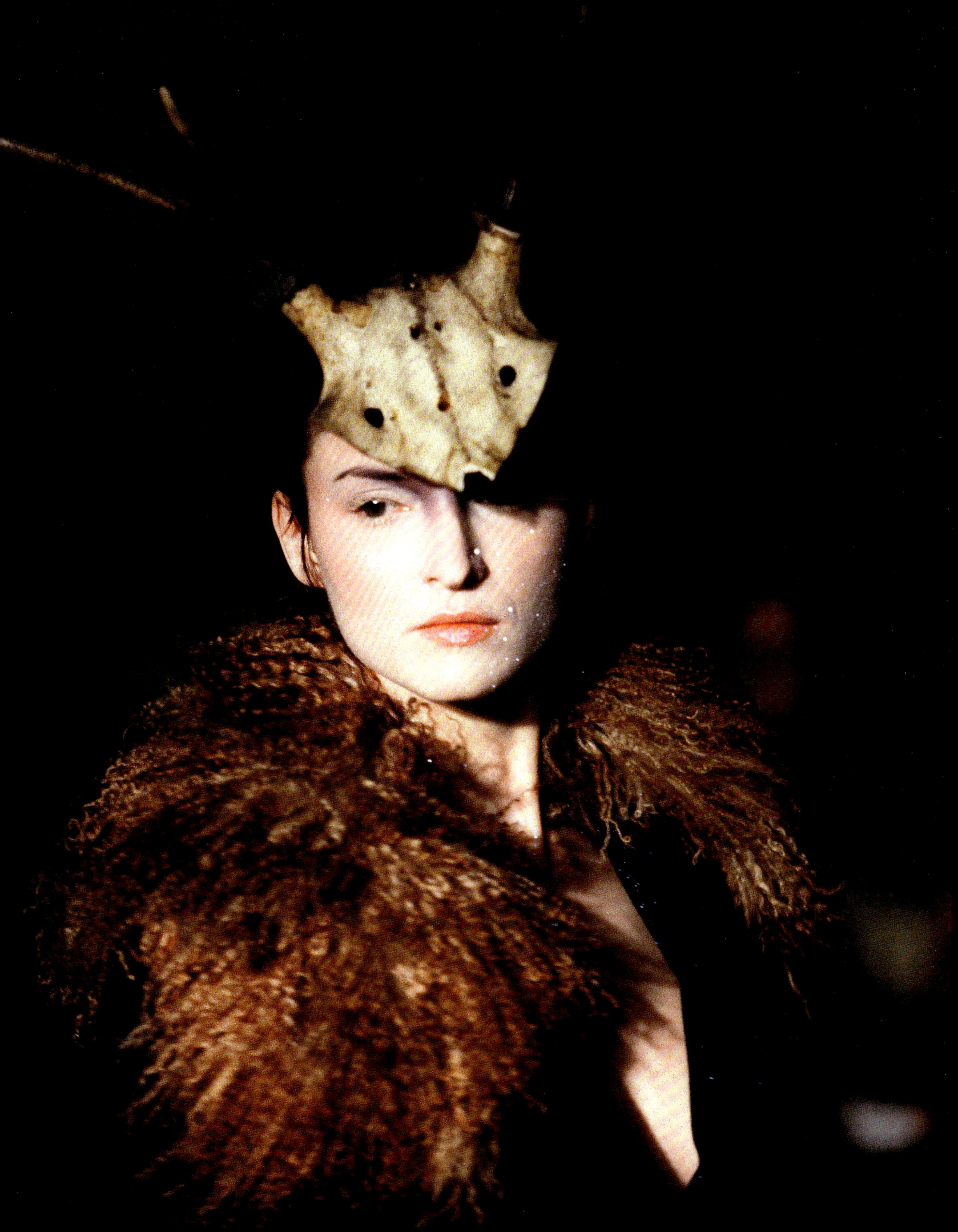

72. *Wax Bodies*, no. 201, 2007. Platinum print. Mannequin from the collection of Evan Michelson. Photograph courtesy Tanya Marcuse.

Vinken drew on philosophers from Hegel to Benjamin to make the case that fashion, like art, has evolved dialectically. Just as it has been suggested elsewhere that Warhol ushered in the age of art after the end of art, so Vinken argued that certain contemporary designers have inaugurated a radically new type of self-reflexive fashion after the end of fashion. As she said, "Fashion today deconstructs the fashion of a hundred years."[63]

It will be recalled how Benjamin argued that fashion has traditionally turned the living woman into a kind of mannequin, "a gaily-decked out corpse." Long an icon of the uncanny, the mannequin is significant to both fashion and the gothic, because it is an abstraction of the corporal body, with, as Vinken puts it, "the soul-less exteriority of the doll." However, the mannequin (doll, automaton, tailor's dummy) plays a new and different role in what Vinken calls "postfashion," because now "all the tricks of the dressmaker are turned out to the light." "Fashion's fascination with the inanimate doll is laid bare – and therefore becomes reversible."[64]

73. Comme des Garçons Spring/Summer 1997. Photograph courtesy Maria Chandoha Valentino.

Instead of disguising its art, fashion now flaunts its artificiality. Consider Rei Kawakubo of Comme des Garçons. Kawakubo not only challenges the social construction of woman as the beautiful sex, she also interrogates the entire idea of fashion. No longer is fashion a false surface that seeks to create the impression of a naturally beautiful female doll. Instead, it exemplifies a new kind of embodiment. In her apparent pursuit of an alternative ideal of beauty, she denaturalizes all our assumptions. The volume of dress may be compressed or stretched or otherwise distorted, as mutable forms imply impossible bodies. Comme des Garçons' famous Dress becomes Body becomes Dress collection of 1997, for example, was

74. (following page) *Dazed & Confused*, August 2007. Clothing by Yohji Yamamoto; boots by Dr. Martens for Yohji Yamamoto. Styling: Katie Shillingford. Photograph courtesy Neil Francis Dawson.

75. (page 71) *Dazed & Confused*, August 2007. Clothing by Yohji Yamamoto; boots by Dr. Martens for Yohji Yamamoto. Styling: Katie Shillingford. Photograph courtesy Neil Francis Dawson.

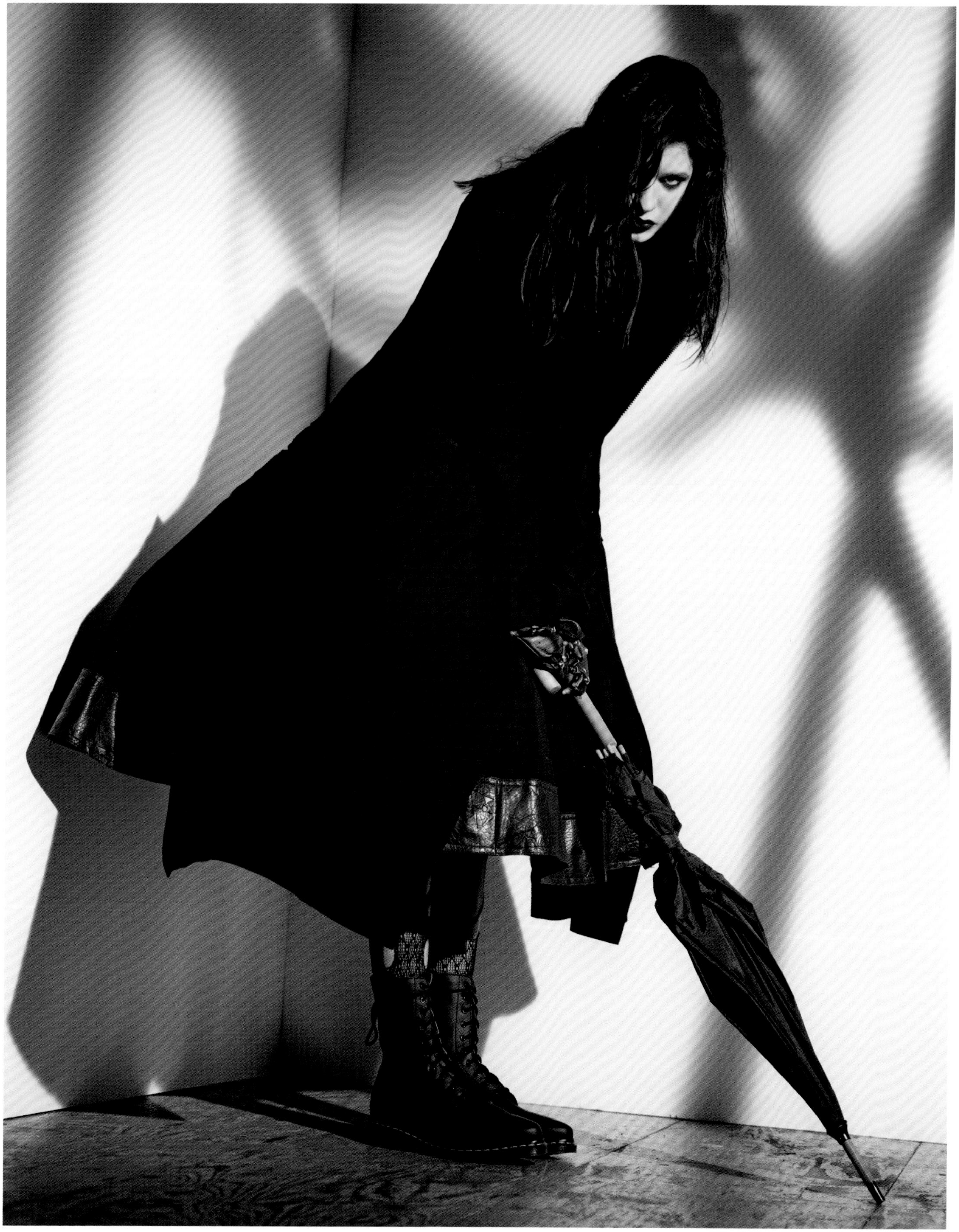

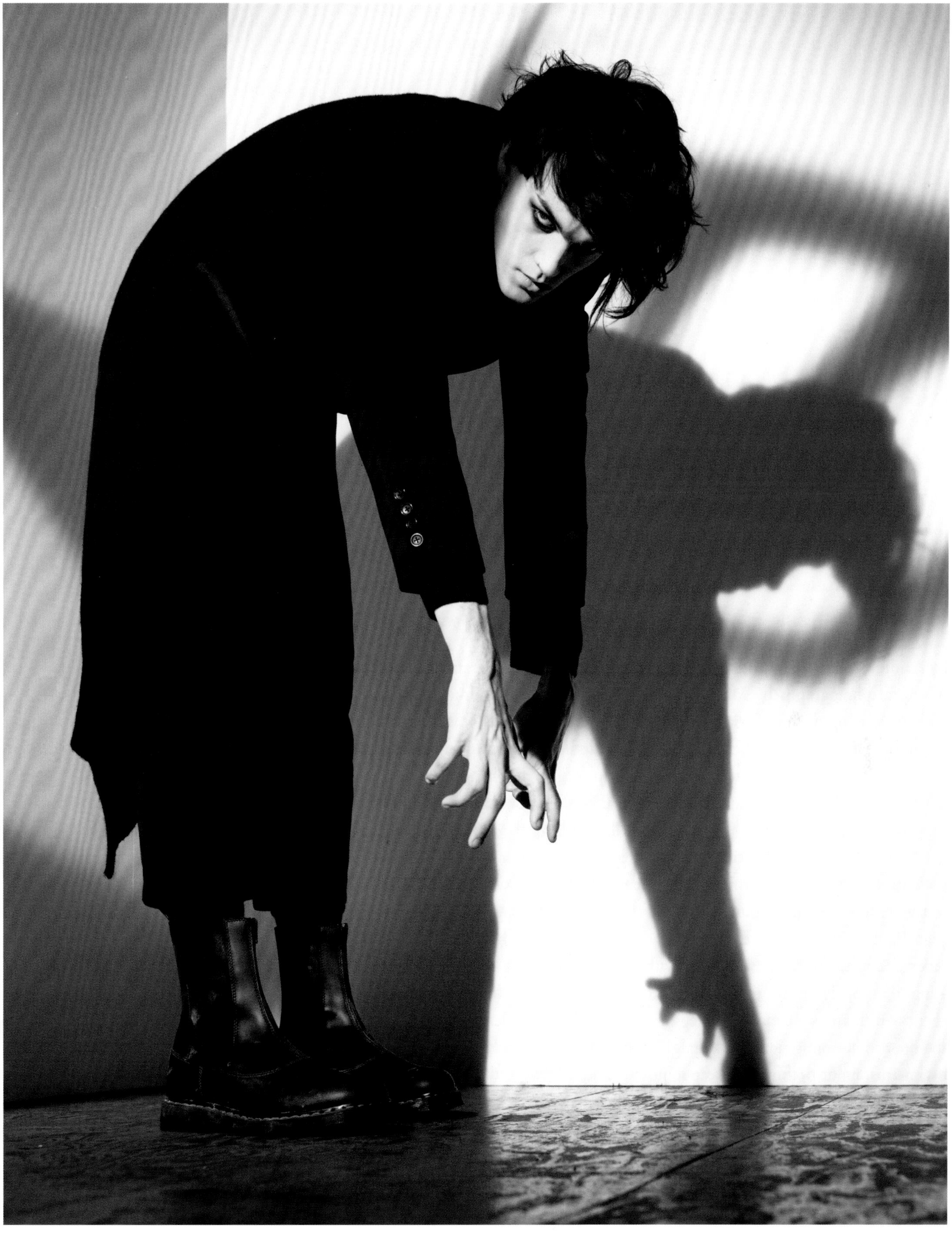

"We are spirits in the material world" declared the caption for another fashion spread, "The Unexplained," also in *The Face* (March 1999). The photographer Lee Jenkins and the stylist Joanna Thaw placed models in ghostly white clothes in a spooky house, where bodies levitated and poltergeists wreaked havok. Fashions by avant-garde designers like Jurgi Persoons, Alexander McQueen, Martin Margiela, and Balenciaga were combined with finds from Portobello Market and the Gallery of Antique Costumes and Textiles.

"Taste of Arsenic" carved out new territory and was correspondingly influential. The young photographer Sean Ellis was approached by *The Face* and asked which stylist he would like to work with. He named Isabella Blow, because he thought it would be interesting to take a high-fashion stylist closely associated with *Vogue* and have her work on a fashion spread for a "street magazine." Their collaboration proved fruitful. "Taste of Arsenic" appeared in the October 1996 issue of *The Face*, and immediately caused a sensation. "Afterwards, Anna Wintour called me, wanting me to do something for Vogue," recalls Ellis. "I wasn't conscious of doing 'Gothic' stuff, but six months later there was a big gothic revival and my style was then described as gothic." The spread featured three young girls wearing high-fashion corsets, a scenario which implicitly emphasized issues of physical restriction and sexual exploitation. One image, for example, shows a young girl, shot slightly from below, dressed in a peculiar collection of garments consisting of a Victorian-style satin corset by the famous corsetier and tight-lacer Mr. Pearl, together with a sleeveless embroidered bolero jacket by Hussein Chalayan, silver high-heeled pumps by Manolo Blahnik, and a tiny skirt by Deborah Milner made out of two skimpy strips of film negatives, which the model lifts and holds out to each side. She resembles a frightened gothic puppet. Made up with a ghostly white face, dark eyes, and wild hair, her crimson mouth is wide open in what looks like a silent scream. Ellis recalls that Isabella Blow had commissioned the skirt especially for the shoot, "as a nod towards my yearning to be a film-maker. I told her that I wanted to make stills for a film that we hadn't made, and Isabella said, 'Let's make a film out of the clothes.'"

Even more famous is "The Clinic," which was also brilliantly photographed by Sean Ellis and styled by Isabella Blow. Also published in *The Face* (March 1997), it depicts an ominous setting of tiled walls and bathroom fixtures resembling a grim mental hospital. "Welcome. We'll tear your soul apart," warns the front-page caption, alluding to the line from the song "We Will Tear Your Soul Apart" by Leviathan. Shadows loom ominously. In one photograph, which has been much reproduced, a figure wearing face jewelry by Shaun Leane for Alexander McQueen appears to be enacting a kind of vampiric penetration of the exposed neck of his dreamily smiling victim. Another photograph shows an eerie, apparently deformed figure reflected in a doorknob, wearing the notorious Distortion Dress by Comme des Garçons.

Yet another photograph, depicts a figure in shadow, appearing to hang from strings like a broken mannequin or the victim of torture. The look of the photographs "came out of the clothes," says Ellis. For example, "Hussein's coat had strings hanging off it, so we yanked the model by the strings. A lot of the

78. (above) "Neverland," *Dazed & Confused*, 1996. Dress by Helmut Lang, gold-plated silver fangs by Naomi Filmer for Hussein Chalayan, Fall/Winter 1996/7. Styling by Alister Mackie. Photograph courtesy Martina Hoogland Ivanow.

79. (facing page) "Taste of Arsenic," *The Face*, October 1996. Gold embroidered bolero by Hussein Chalayan, satin corset by Pearl, tortoiseshell film-strip skirt by Deborah Milner. Styling by Isabella Blow. Photograph courtesy Sean Ellis/www.theofficelondon.com.

80. (page 76) "The Clinic: Welcome. We'll tear your soul apart," *The Face,* March 1997. Jacket by Hussein Chalayan, knickers by Alexander McQueen. Styling by Isabella Blow. Photograph courtesy Sean Ellis/www.theofficelondon.com.

81. (page 77) Finger horns by Sarah Harmanee for Alexander McQueen, *It's a Jungle Out There*, Fall/Winter 1997/8. Styling by Isabella Blow. Photograph courtesy Sean Ellis/ www.theofficelondon.com.

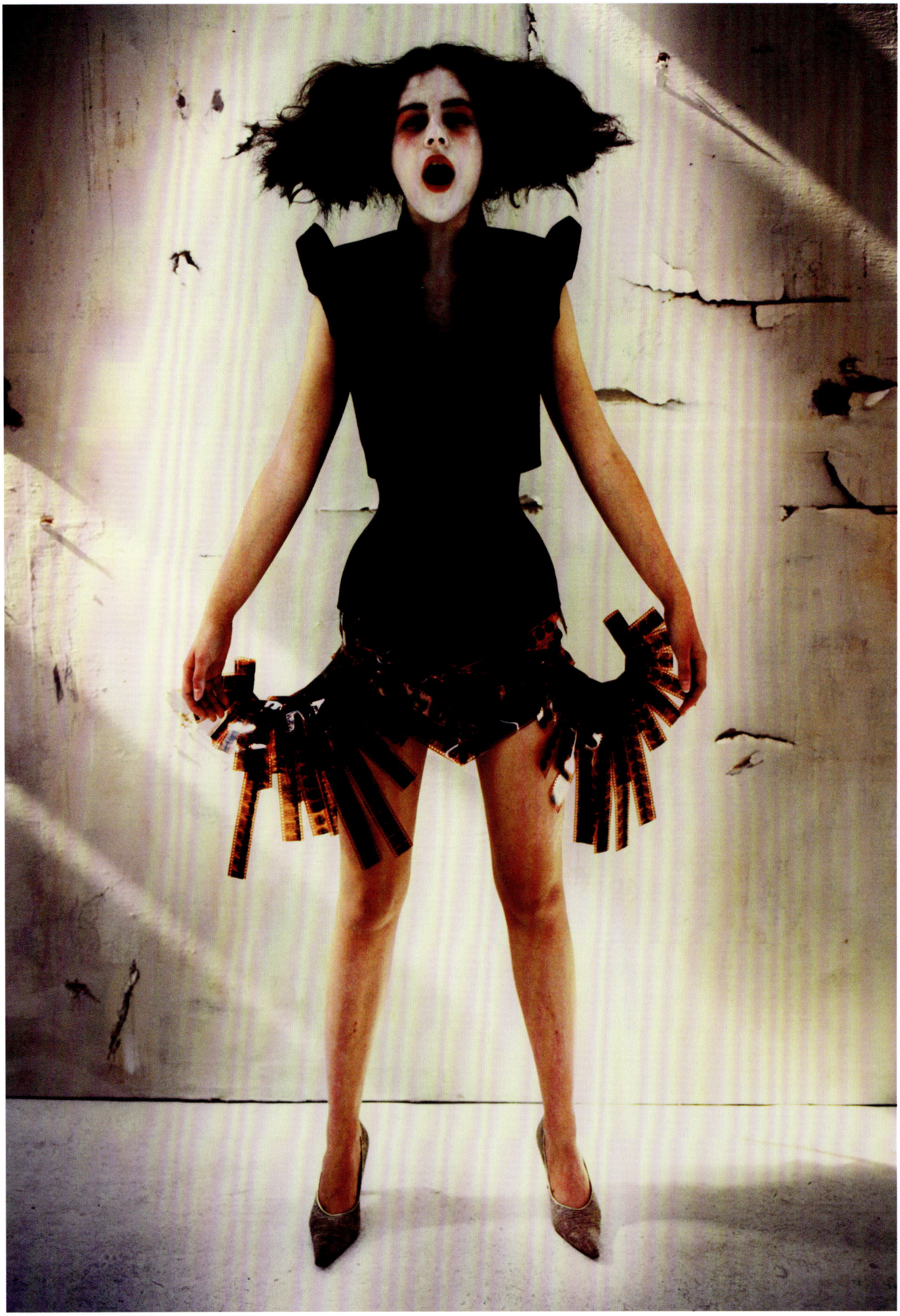

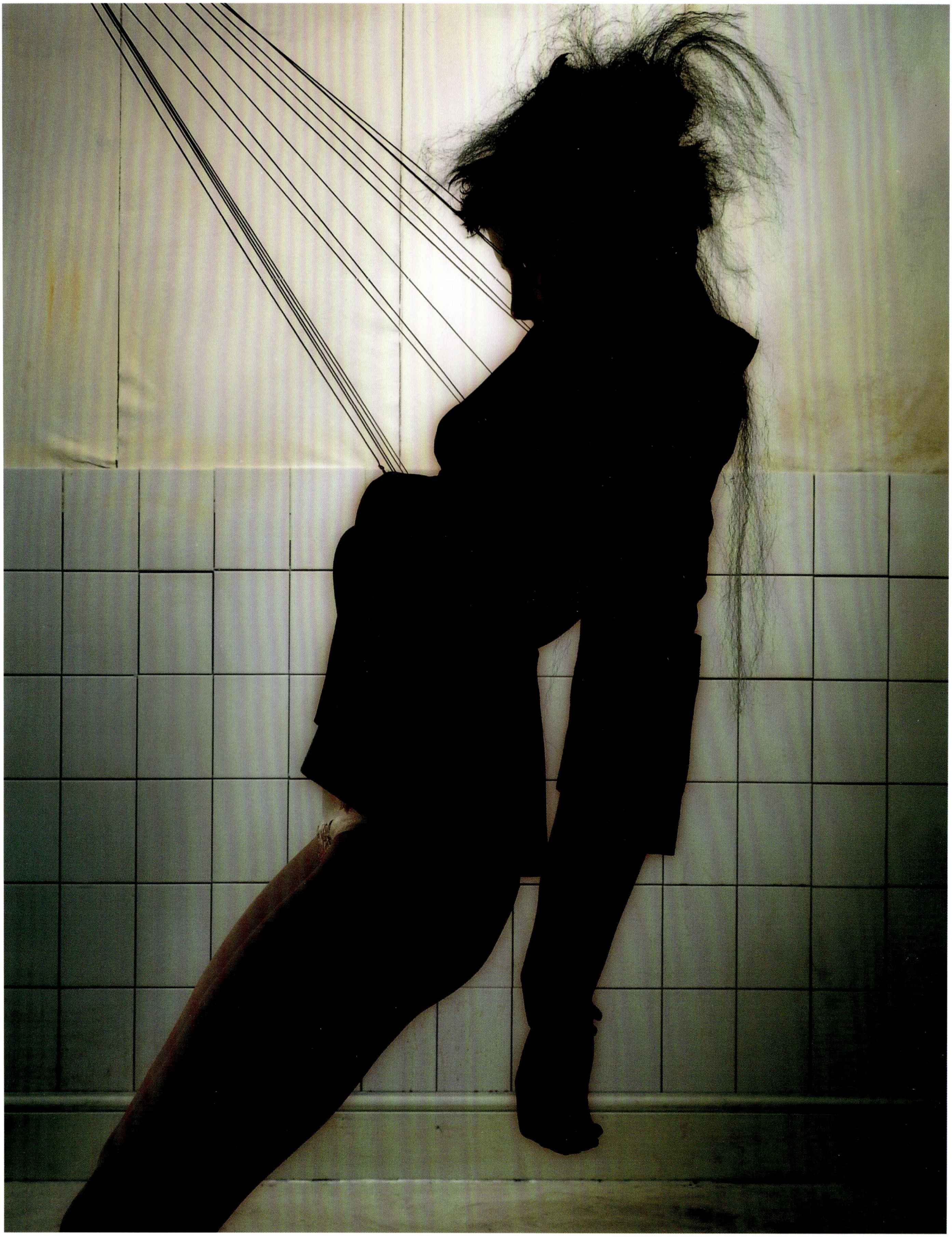

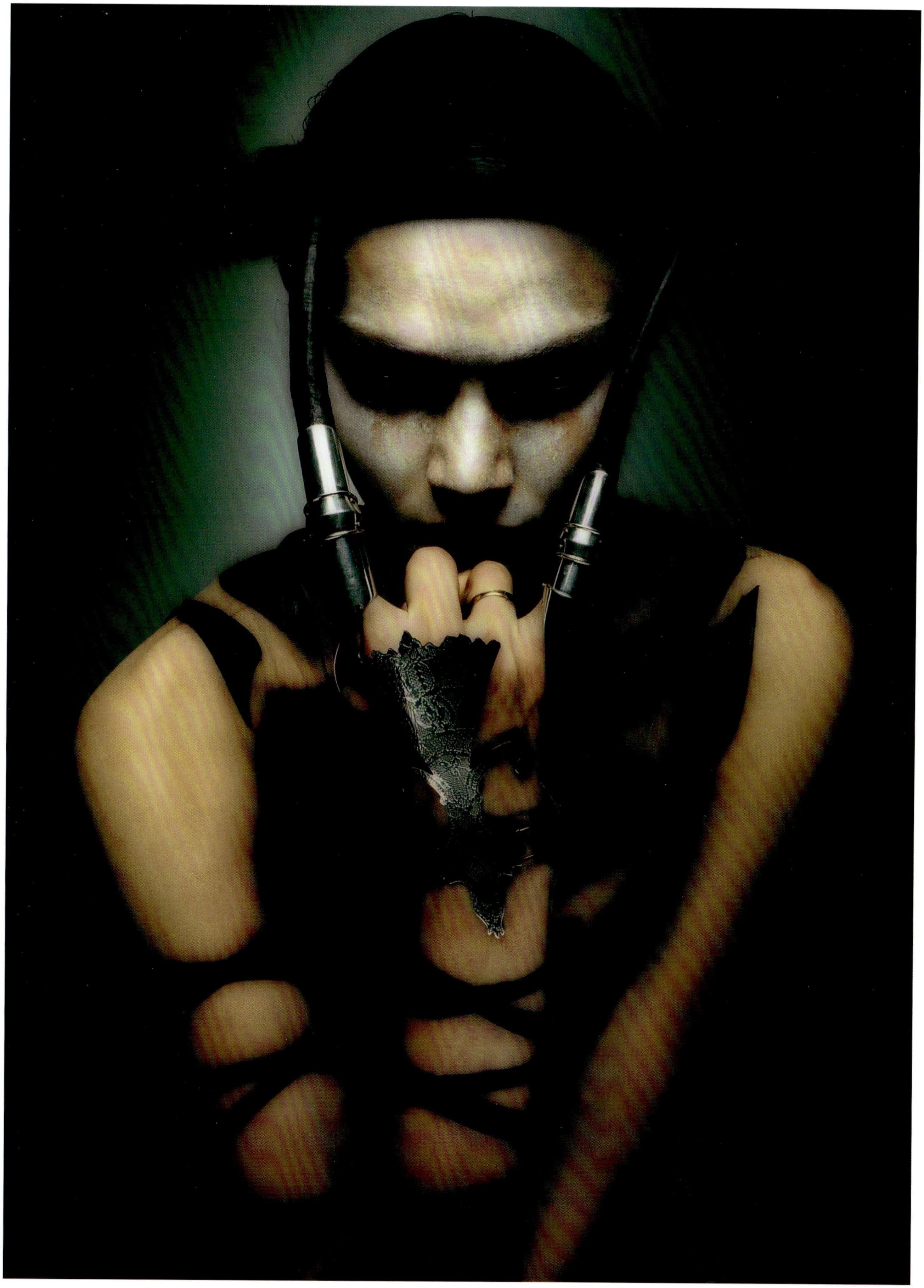

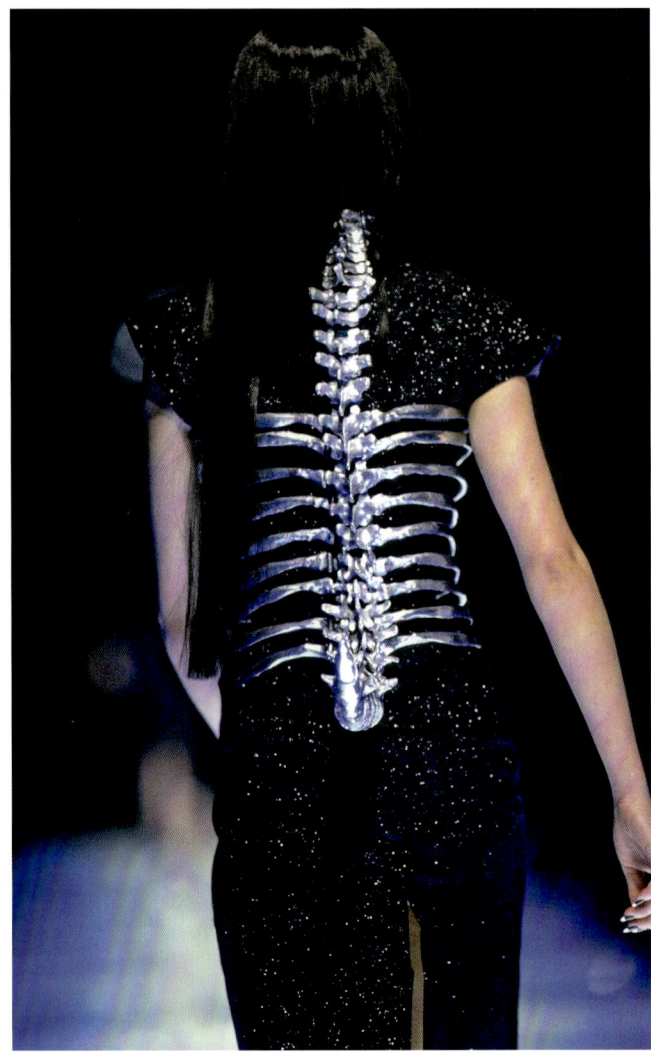

skulls, and condor talons. His sketches also contributed to McQueen's vision for the *Eclect/Dissect* collection in 1997.

The master of fashion theatre, John Galliano, often draws on gothic themes. His Spring/Summer 2006 collection for Christian Dior Haute Couture, for example, was replete with ghostly make-up, blood-red dresses, and gigantic crosses. Galliano has also been inspired by medieval images of the *danse macabre* depicting death as a skeleton. When I asked John Galliano, "What does 'Gothic' mean to you?" he replied, "dark, vampy, mysterious, dangerous – she is edgy and cool. The gothic girl weaves a web, has a sting in her tail, is inspired by black magic and voodoo . . . She is the one that opens Pandora's Box, and to hell with the consequences! She is tantalizing, after-dark trouble that dresses in the shadows of the night." [71]

In gothic narratives, the architectural setting is often symbolic of the human mind, "psychology in stone." According to the scholar Chris Baldick, a gothic work "should combine a fearful sense of inheritance in time with a claustrophobic sense of enclosure in space, these two dimensions reinforcing one another to produce an impression of sickening descent into disintegration." [72] If fashion

88. (left) Alexander McQueen, *What a Merry-go-Round*, Fall/Winter 2001/2. Photograph: Roberto Tecchio. Courtesy Roberto Tecchio and Judith Clark.

89. (right) Ribcage corset by Shaun Leane for Alexander McQueen, Spring/Summer 1998. Photograph courtesy Chris Moore.

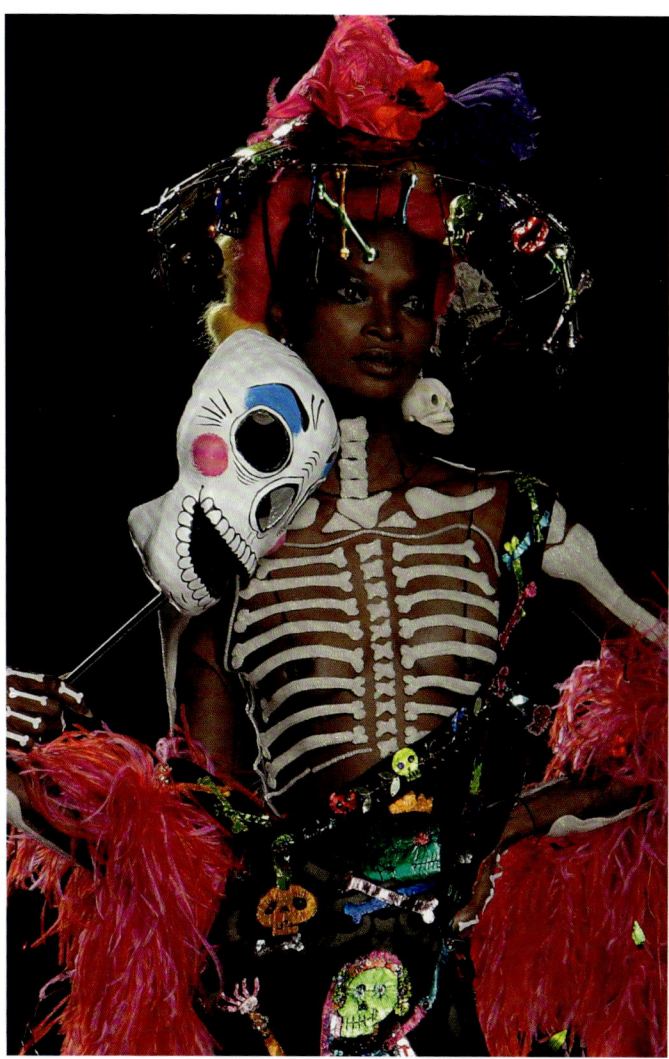

may be considered a type of "intimate architecture," then one might expect gothic fashions to manifest similar characteristics of imprisonment, ambiguity, and disintegration. Certainly, this is seen on occasion, especially with respect to the *mise-en-scene* within which gothic fashion is presented. Consider Alexander McQueen's brilliant yet disturbing Spring/Summer 2001 fashion show, *Voss*.

The audience was seated around a giant mirrored box, which morphed into glass walls. Into this "lunatic asylum setting" entered the models. "At first, the only signs of derangement were in the gauze-bandaged heads," reported the fashion journalist Suzy Menkes; "Then came the gusts of manic laughter, the hands clawing at the cell windows . . . And always there was the ghostly fluttering in the sealed central box. Its walls finally shattered to release a plague of giant moths" – surrounding the grotesque nude figure of an obese woman. Like an artist, McQueen explored some of the same themes addressed that season in the art exhibition "Apocalypse: Beauty and Horror" at London's Royal Academy. Acclaiming McQueen's "superb" show of "ravishing clothes," Menkes was still forced to ask: "How far should a designer delve into the mirror of our vanities to explore the dark horrors behind an immaculate appearance?"[73]

90. (left) John Galliano for Christian Dior Haute Couture Spring/Summer 2006. Photograph courtesy Maria Chandoha Valentino.

91. (right) John Galliano for Christian Dior Haute Couture Fall/Winter 2000/1. Photograph courtesy Maria Chandoha Valentino.

92. (following pages) Alexander McQueen, *Voss*, Spring/Summer 2001. Photograph courtesy Chris Moore.

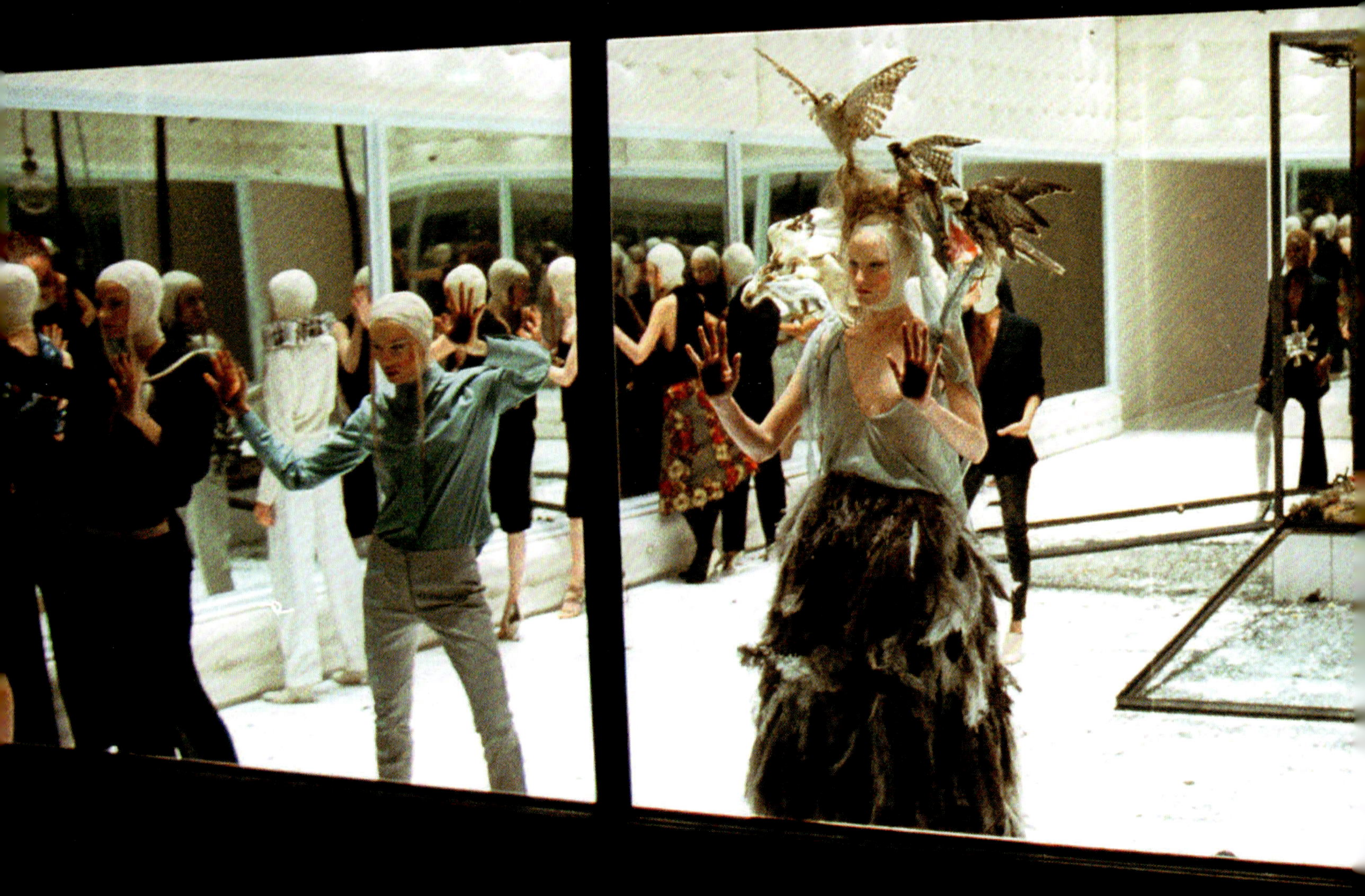

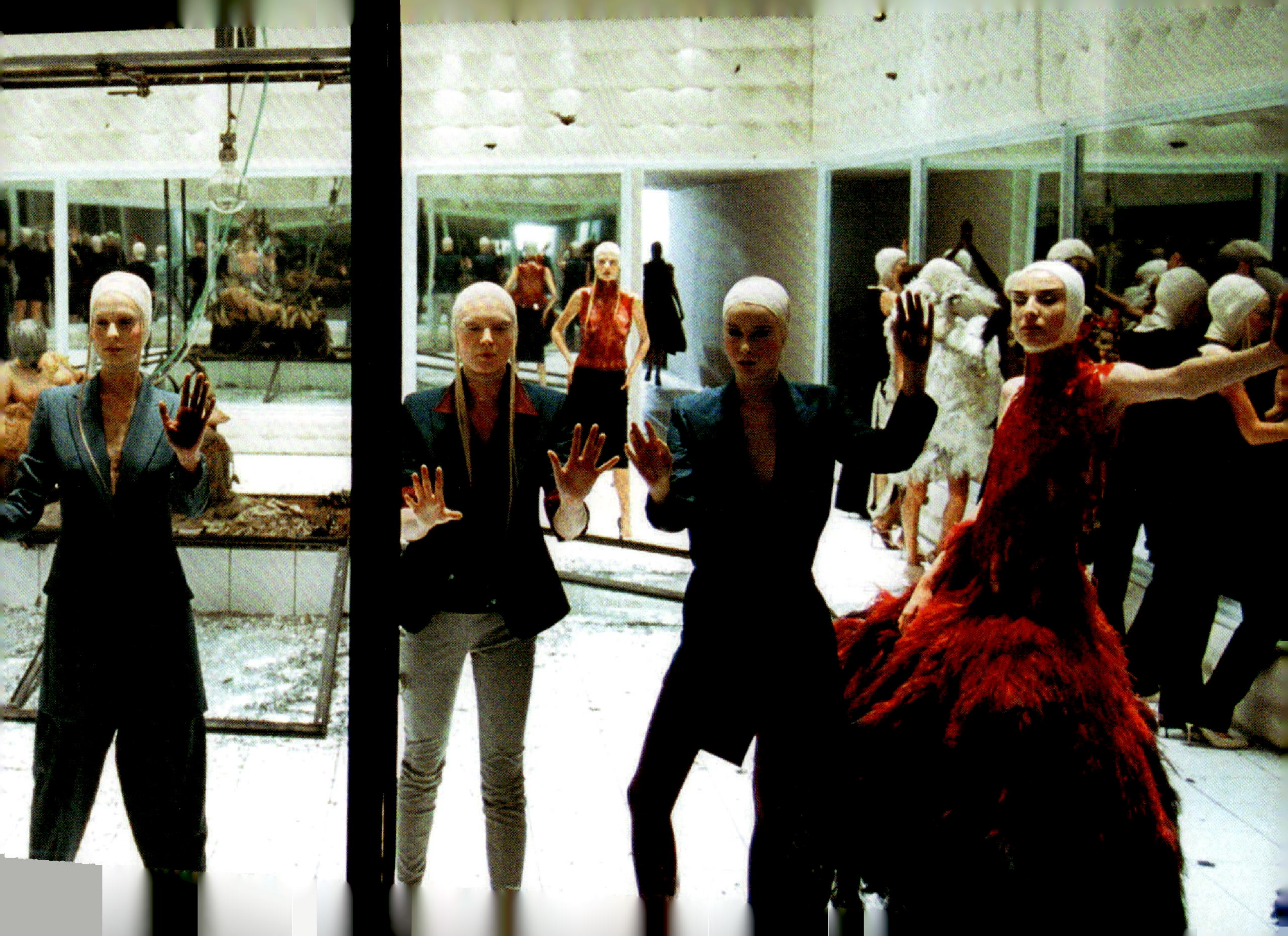

McQueen's mirrored asylum is a reminder that fashion as a phenomenon inevitably emphasizes surface, spectacle, and performance. This, too, is part of the gothic.

Galliano, in particular, has developed an array of extraordinary dramatic personae. His Spring/Summer 1998 collection for Christian Dior Haute Couture, for example, was inspired by the Marchesa Casati, whose lurid make-up and eccentric fashions thrilled Europe in the early twentieth century. When I asked Galliano why he was intrigued by Casati, he said that he hardly knew "where to start: her life, her passion, her style, her attitude . . . She was and remains the ultimate celebrity *femme fatale* – fascinating!"

"I want to be a living work of art," declared Casati, and so she was, albeit a weird, macabre masterpiece. Pale and emaciated, her enormous eyes drugged with belladonna and encircled with kohl, always fantastically arrayed with jewels and "shining crosses," she personified the idea of decadence. Naturally, she was an enthusiast for the occult and séances. Arthur Rubenstein actually screamed the first time he saw her, because she looked so much like a ghost. The Italian socialite Dora di Rudini also had a bizarre encounter at Casati's house. Arriving, she found

93. (above) Michelle Olley modeling for Alexander McQueen, *Voss*, Spring/Summer 2001. Photograph courtesy Chris Moore.

94. (facing page) Simon Costin, Memento Mori necklace, 1986. Ruined Victorian jet, rhinestones, wooden beads, rabbit skulls, and condor talons. Courtesy Simon Costin. Photograph: Simon Brown.

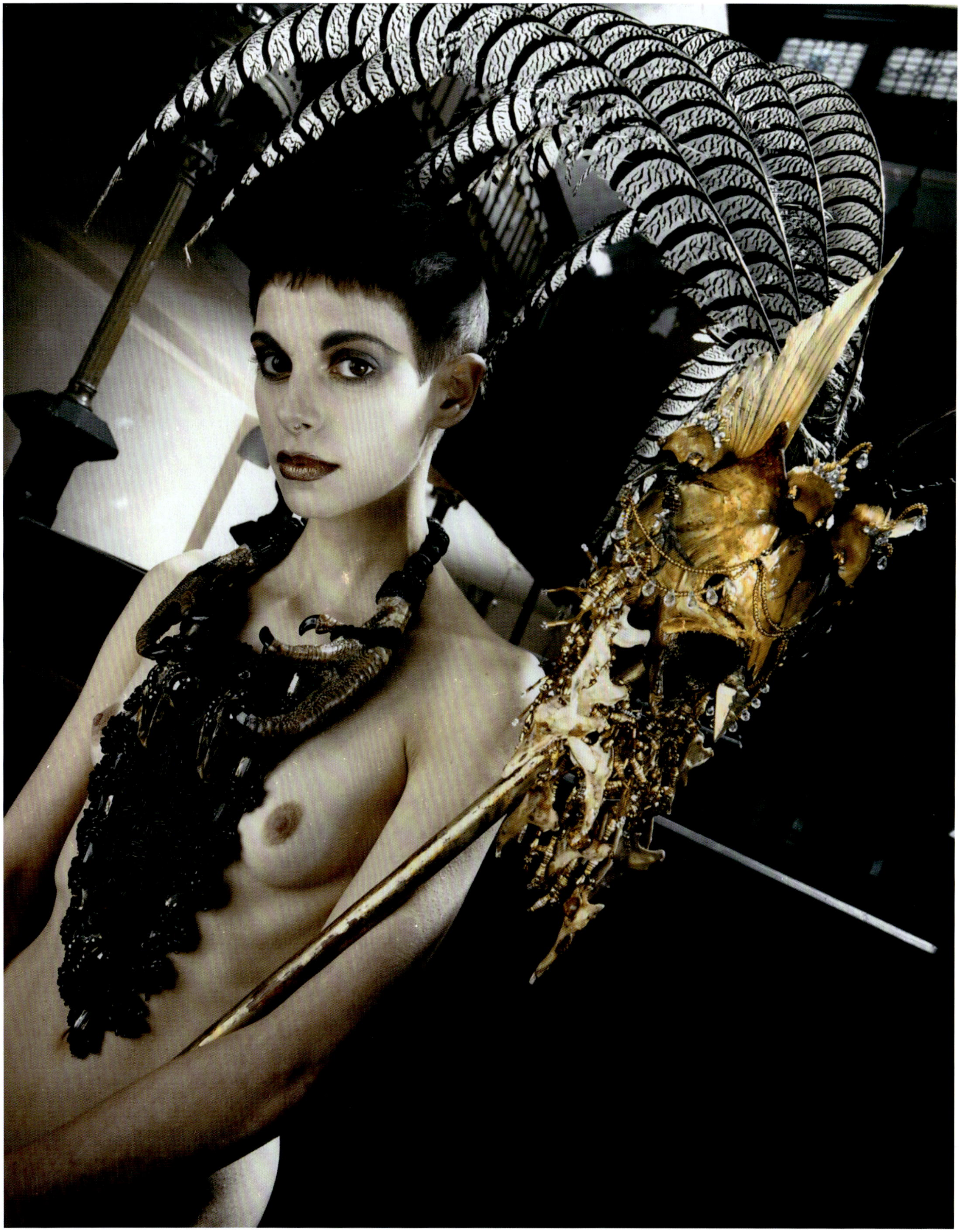

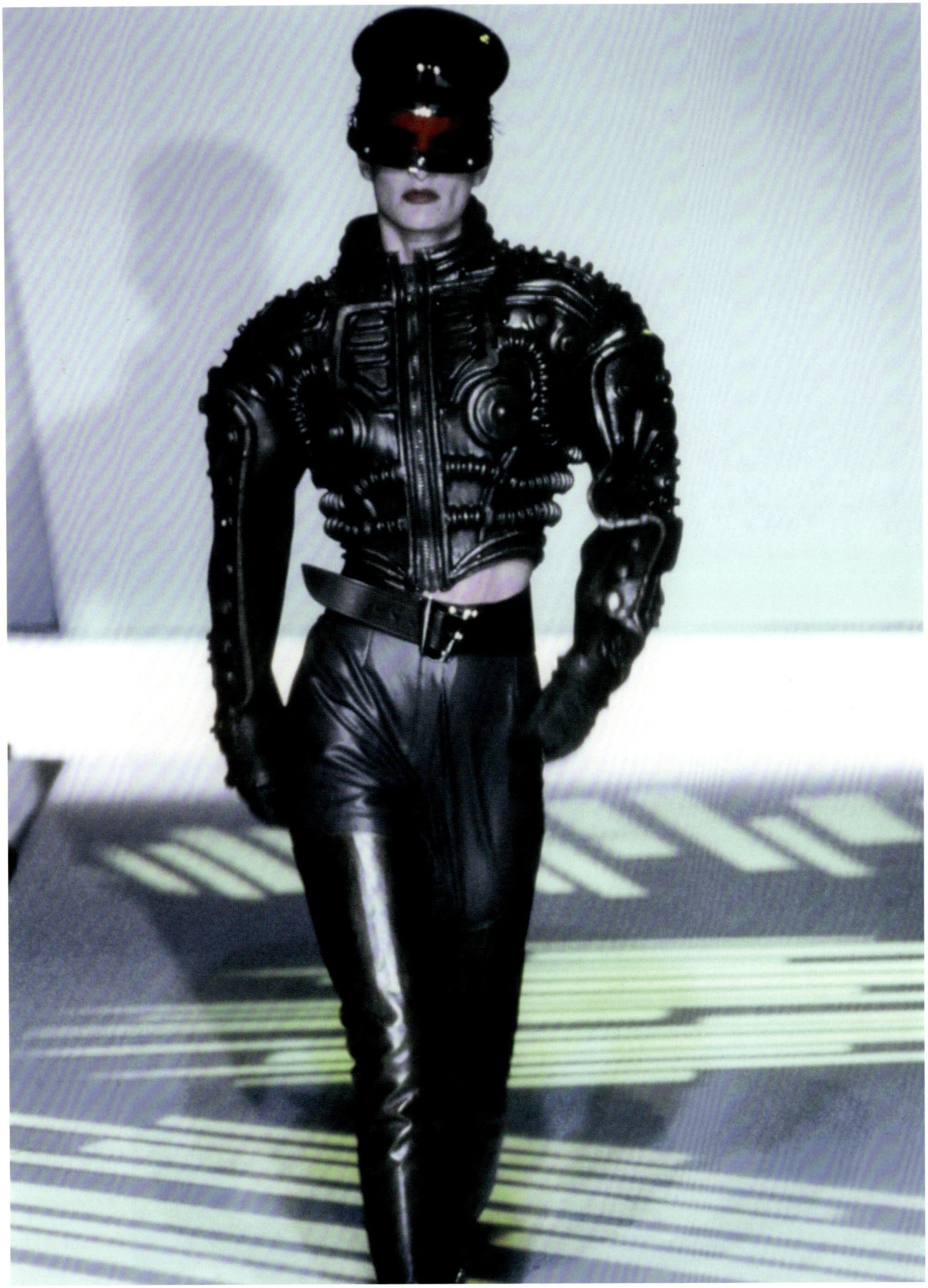

Owens's inspiration, Thierry Mugler, one of fashion's greatest fantasists, has been strongly influenced by the iconography of sexual fetishism. Indeed, Mugler has created a veritable gallery of fetish fashions, some of which allude to the gothic figure of the vampire. Simon Doonan took up the theme in a window display at Barneys, featuring a Mugler-clad mannequin in a coffin. Mugler has also drawn on the image of the sexy robot, a theme that extends from the film *Metropolis* to the dress of cyber goths, and which recalls key gothic texts such as *Frankenstein*.

Men's fashion, too, has been influenced by "the dark side," a theme explored throughout an entire issue of the magazine *Fashion, Inc.* (Autumn 2006), in which articles and fashion spreads carried titles such as "Prince of Darkness" (about Alexander McQueen), "L'Homme Fatal" (about Hedi Slimane, at that time menswear designer for Christian Dior), "Devil is in the Details," "The Hunger," and "Le Chic, C'est Gothique". The magazine's cover image by Perry Hagopian depicted a young man with long black hair wearing a black ruffled

107. (facing page) Thierry Mugler Ready-to-Wear Fall/Winter 1991/2. Photograph: Patrice Stable. Courtesy Thierry Mugler.

108. (above) Simon Doonan's Halloween Vampire Scenario with clothing by Thierry Mugler, Barneys, 17th Street, New York, 1989. Photograph © Barneys New York, courtesy Simon Doonan.

shirt by Gucci, black leather jeans, and a pleated leather cummerbund by Giles Rosier. In menswear, black "comes with an attitude: 'I wear black, don't fuck with me,'" declared Mark C. O'Flaherty in his article "Black Magic" (2006). After emphasizing the important of Japanese avant-garde designers, whose clothes appealed to architects and intellectuals, he observed that "wearing black was also seized upon by the dreaded goths who were nothing if not the miserabilist children of the beatniks... Menswear designers from McQueen to Cloak have consistently borrowed from the goths..."[83]

Styling throughout the issue emphasized various aspects of the sinister, such as death, vampires, blood, and ghosts. Interviewees, however, paid little or no attention to this subject matter. Asked about his Spring/Summer 2007 menswear show, McQueen said only, "Lots of vampires, wasn't it?" adding "We followed the narrative from Coppola's film version of Dracula." Questioned about his style, he replied: "I'm always dark but I've been darker."[84] Meanwhile, Hedi Slimane, who launched a major trend for slim-cut black suits, recalled that "The first image of menswear that I saw was an album cover of David Bowie at age six."[85]

Skull imagery has been an especially noticeable theme in menswear, especially since 2006. Influential trendsetters were Comme des Garçons and McQueen, although the graffitti artist Banksy had already created memorable images of a smiley-face skeleton. The skull look was rapidly picked up for street wear aimed at the young urban consumer. Skulls appeared on hoodies, T-shirts, baseball caps, and rhinestone belt buckles. If men carried skeleton keychains, women adopted skull necklaces. By 2007 the skull image was so ubiquitous that it could be seen on little dog coats. The artist Damien Hirst created a multi-million-dollar diamond-encrusted skull that became even more notorious than his dead shark artwork: "The Impossibility of Death in the Mind of Someone Living."

Throughout the past two decades, press coverage has spiked every time the goth look seemed to rise from the dead. Much of the press was negative in tone. "The Return of Goth?" found Ashley Heath complaining about the "black shrouds" on the Paris catwalks in 1993.[86] "Grimly Fiendish" suggested that, while goth might be "making a comeback" in mid-1990s America, "in Britain it has never gone away." Recycling popular clichés, the author Emma Forrest complained that "Goths are passive rebels, compared to punks who are energetic and outward." She also underlined goth's negative association with femininity: "For adolescent girls, the pull towards all things black velvet and mystical is especially strong."[87]

Since fashion discourse habitually denigrates the recent past in order to celebrate the latest style, it is not surprising that journalists have tended to take a predictable position on the "return of goth." While admitting to elements of the past style, they usually insist that this new incarnation is different and much better. "They're back, they're all in black, but this time goth girls are ... not wearing fishnets," declared British *Elle* in 1995. The "New Goths" were said to be "More vamp than vampire, sexy not spooky," and definitely "Not to be confused with Punk or The Rocky Horror Show Look." Visuals accompanying the article included a stylish black cross by Lalique, a bottle of black nail polish, a picture of Uma

109. (facing page) Photograph by Perry Hagopian, featured on the cover of *Fashion, Inc.* Autumn 2006. Courtesy Perry Hagopian.

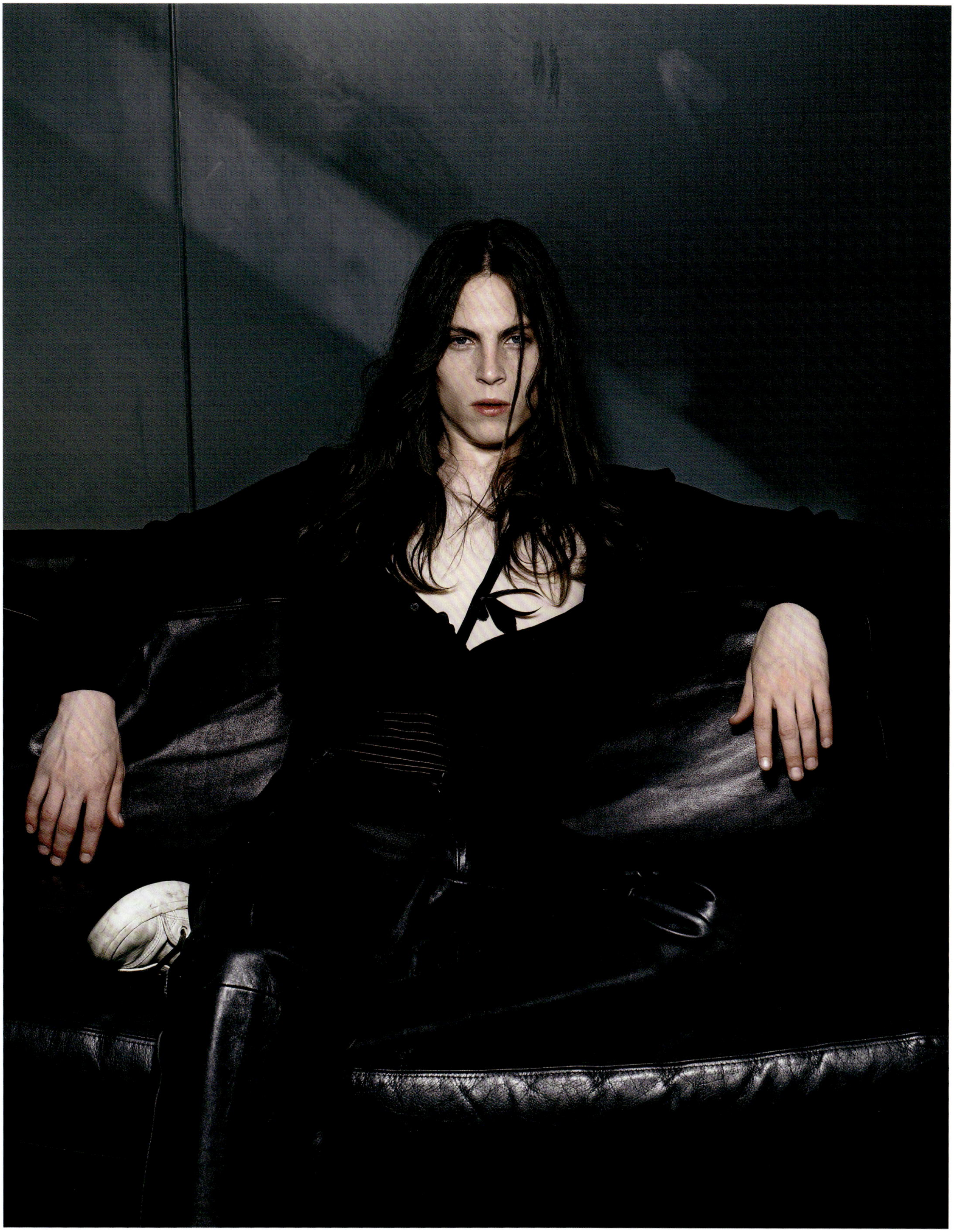

rag-picker, so also does the suturing together of these fragments bring to mind the unholy creation of monsters like Frankenstein. Of course, deconstruction has long since been appropriated by couture, but even at its most elegant, it still conveys a certain violence. Laura and Kate Mulleavy of Rodarte, for example, were inspired by Japanese horror films to create cobwebby, distressed gothic looks.

Rei Kawakubo's famous Lace Sweater was made by adjusting the knitting machine so that it created a sweater full of holes. Although her approach differed significantly from the aggression inherent in the torn clothing of the punks and the love of ruins espoused by the goths, all of them have been ineluctably drawn toward the dissolution of form. This theme, in turn, recalls a story told by Barbey d'Aurevilly, which may be apochryphal, of dandyism in the time of Beau Brummell. "Incredible though it may seem, the Dandies once had a fancy for *torn clothes*," wrote d'Aurevilly:

> They had come to the end of impertinences and were at a loss how to proceed, when they hit upon this dandiesque idea, which was, to have their clothes torn, before wearing them, through the whole extent of the cloth, until it was nothing more than a sort of lace – a cloud! They wanted to walk like Gods

115. (left) Hussein Chalayan, "Fifties Edwardian Corset Dress," *Medea* collection, Spring/Summer 2002. Photograph: Chris Moore. Courtesy Hussein Chalayan.

116. (right) Rodarte, Fall/Winter 2008–9. Photograph: Dan Lecca. Courtesy Rodarte.

117. (facing page) Gattinoni Couture Fall/Winter 1997/8. Photograph: Antonio Barrella. Courtesy Atelier Gattinoni.

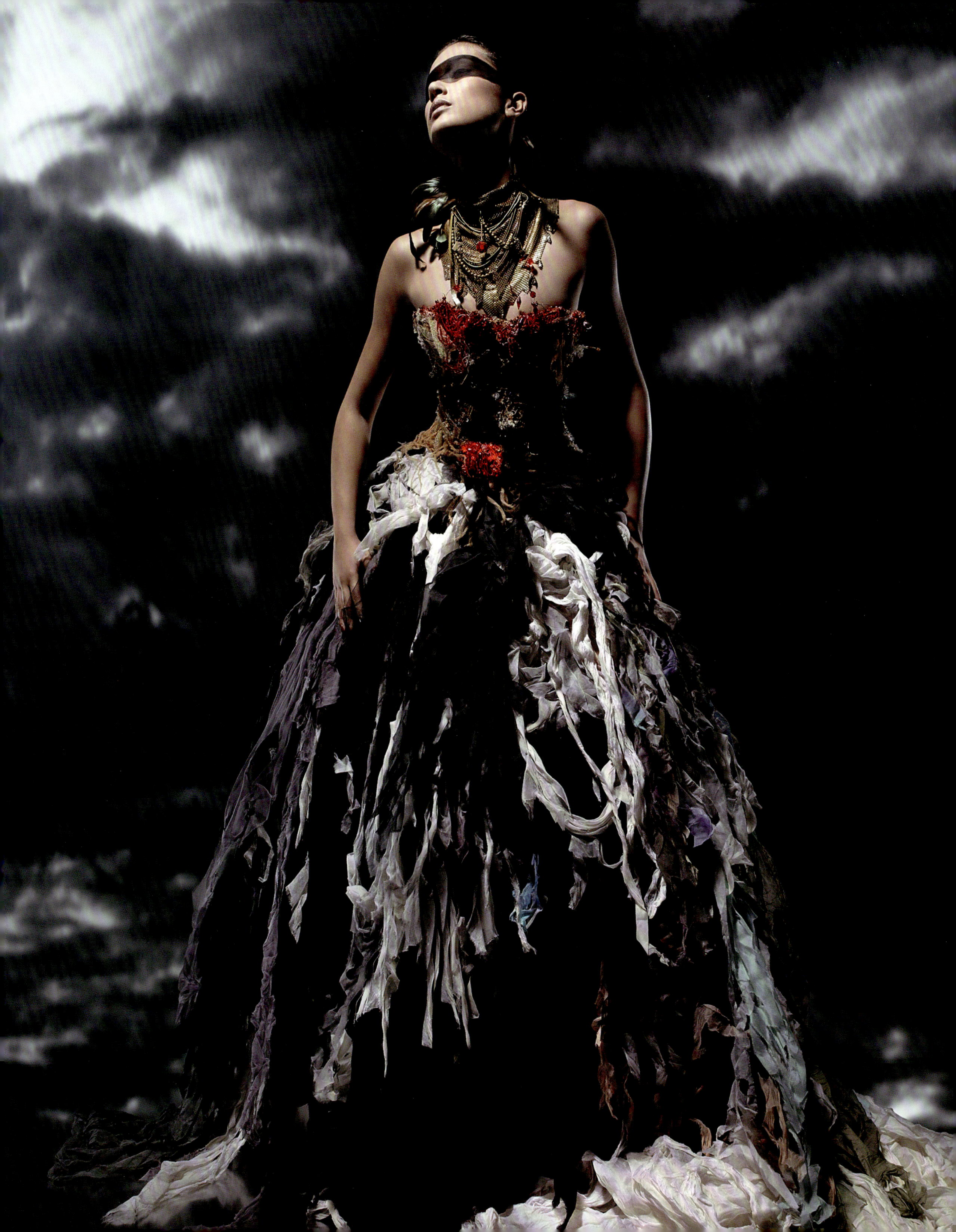

118. Dai Rees, Mask, 1998. Sheep's pelvis, Czech crystal, Swarovski crystal, silver. Photograph: Mat Collishaw. From *Pampilion*, exhibition catalogue, Judith Clark Costume Gallery, 1998. Courtesy Judith Clark Costume.

in their clouds! The operation was difficult and tedious to execute, and to accomplish it they used a bit of sharpened glass. And, well, there's a true example of Dandyism! The clothes themselves are not important. They practically no longer *exist*.[92]

It is sometimes argued that young people, such as goths, deal with feelings of alienation by fashioning themselves as exotic monsters. Discussions have tended to focus on whether they are "sincere" about their self-created identities or whether they are just "faking it." Is their clothing only a superficial form of "gothic chic" or is it "an authentic expression of the 'Gothic psyche'"?[93] This paradigm of mirror versus mask seems inherently unsatisfactory, however. The fetishization of "authenticity" does not take account of the fact that clothing can never "mirror" an essential, inner self, since that self does not exist. Even if we think we are being most "natural" and "sincere," we are still creating a persona – just as much as if we wore a mask by Dai Rees or styled ourselves like the aliens who have appeared on the runway of the young British designer Gareth Pugh.

Gothic fashion, like the gothic novel, tends to be obsessed with the past, often a theatrical, highly artificial version of the past that contrasts dramatically with

119. (facing page) Gareth Pugh Fall/Winter 2006/7. Courtesy Gareth Pugh.

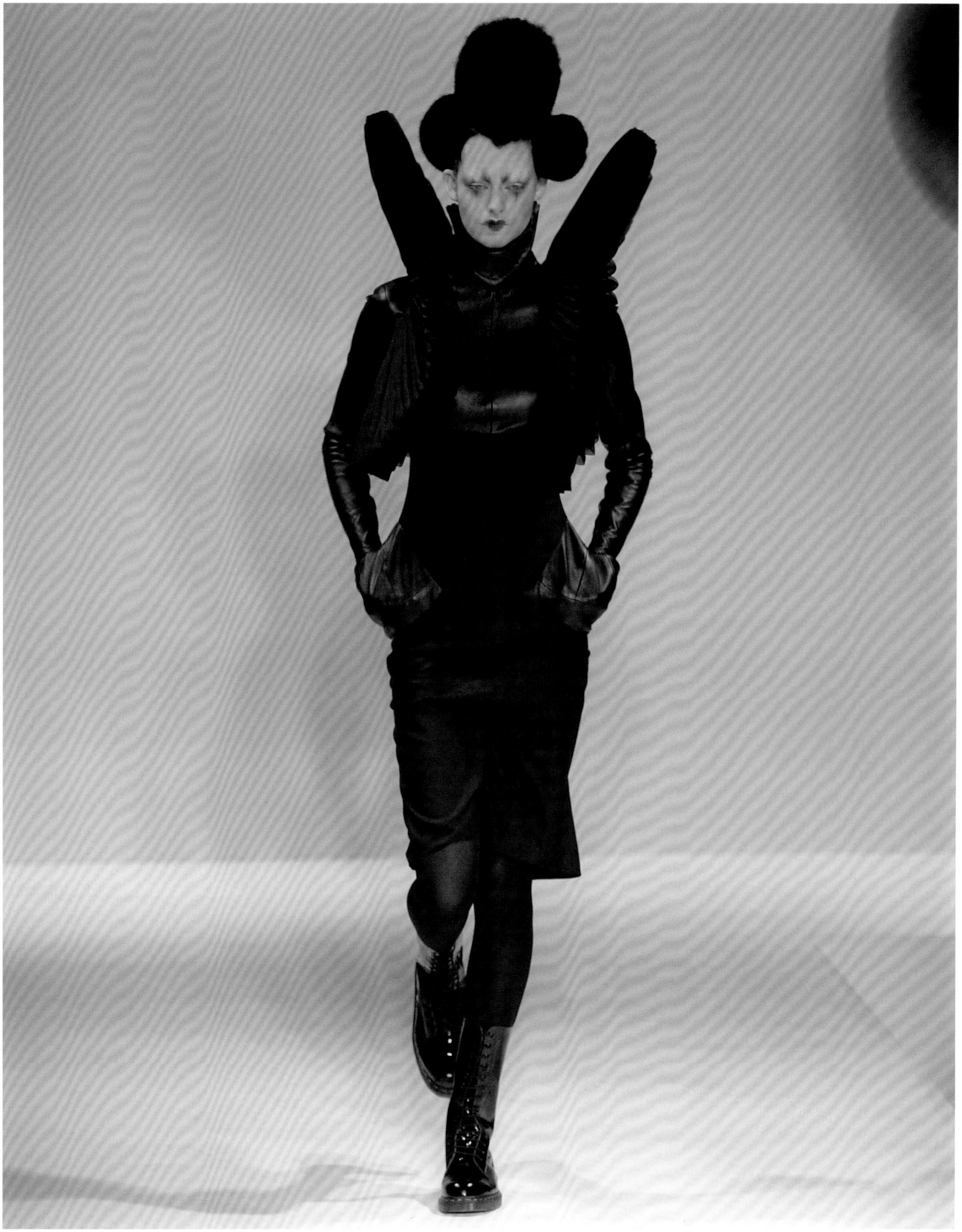

Harrison, who appreciated the moralistic image of the harpies Fashion and Vanity lacing a corset. To the original caption, *à la mode à la mort* (fashionable to the death), was added another Victorian anti-corset cliché: "Assassin of the Human Race." "As for the future of Goth style, there is one new look emerging that may become incorporated into the Goth wardrobe," says Julia Borden. "The Gothic Steam Punk look, originating in Seattle and Portland. Steam Punk is a splinter genre of Cyberpunk literature that concerns itself with Victoriana. The Steam Punk look is one of the Victorian dandy, the Victorian tradesman, the lady of flight, all filtered

124. (left) Jane Wildgoose, design for female cenobite costume in *Hellraiser* (New World Films 1987). © Jane Wildgoose, 1986.

125. (top) Jane Wildgoose, Mourning Bride Dress, 1984. Designed, printed, cut, and made by Jane Wildgoose, for a party at James Hodgson's house, London, 1984. Photograph: Paul Henry. Courtesy Jane Wildgoose.

126. (above) Kambriel, Midnight Bustle Dress, worn by Lilah. Photograph: Nadya Lev. Courtesy Kambriel.

127. (facing page) Steam Punk ensemble with vintage army surplus pieces, worn by Lisette. Photograph courtesy Kat Bret.

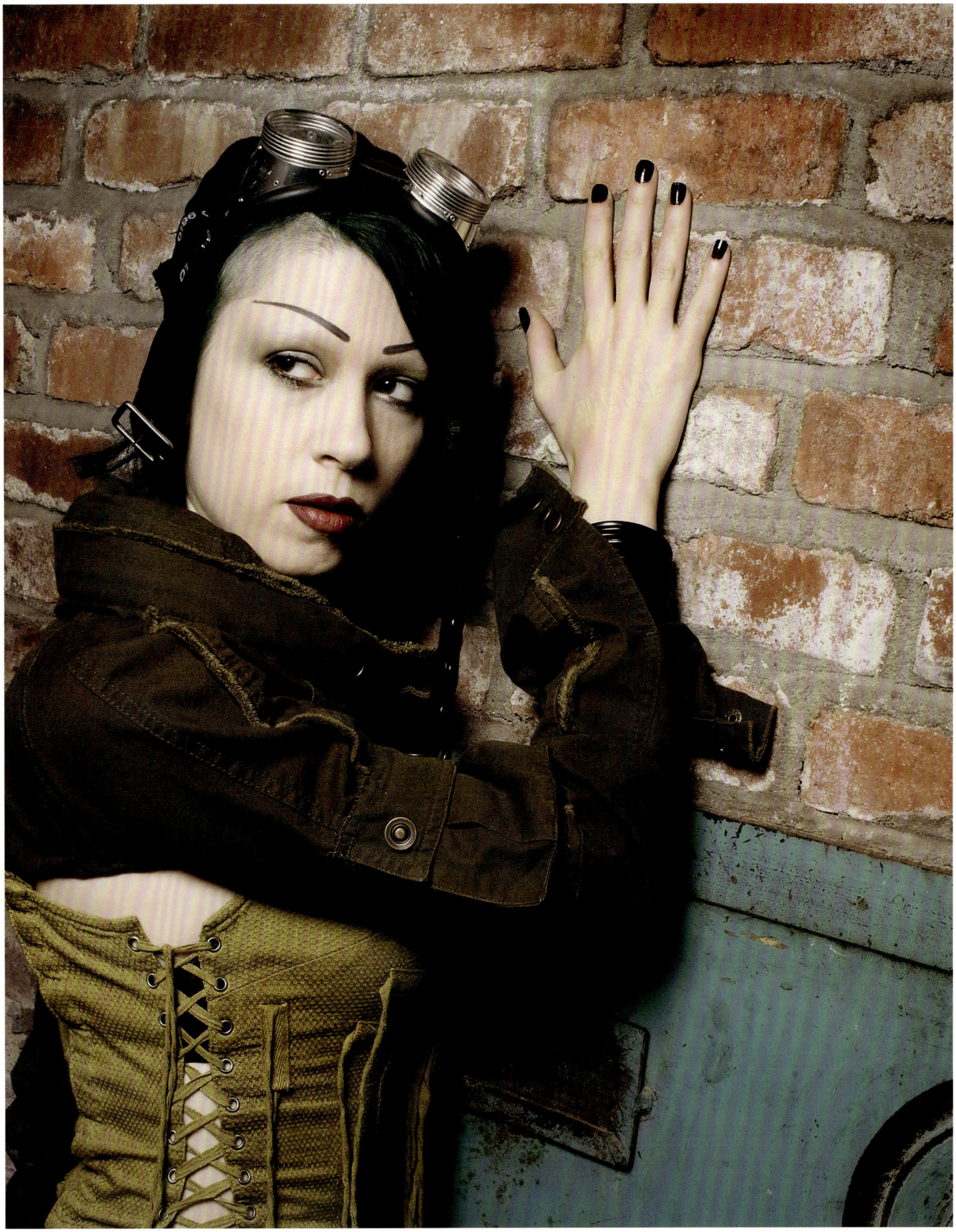

through industrial steam technology and Punk. Antique goggles worn on top hats, women in flight caps with the straps hanging down, Victorian-style clothing in heavy black canvas and leather . . . ".[95] Steam Punk is not a nostalgic evocation of upper-class neo-Victoriana, but rather an aesthetic technological movement with anarchist undertones, linking punk's aggressive do-it-yourself ethic with an evocation of an ancestral gallery of absinth addicts, dandies, and mad inventors. As *Steampunk Magazine* puts it: "Our corsets are stitched with safety pins and our top hats hide vicious Mohawks. We are fashion's jackals running wild in the tailor shop."[96]

As a genre, the gothic is characterized by the themes of death, destruction, and decay, haunting and imprisonment, the powers of horror, and the erotic macabre. Gothic fashion is also linked to a particular sensibility, usually a kind of dark romanticism. It has its own visual vocabulary which evolved from a set of narrative associations evoked by the gothic literature of terror, from its origin in the eighteenth century to its contemporary manifestations in vampire fiction, cinema, and art. Within the world of fashion, the gothic look is perhaps most clearly expressed in the form of photography. I have shown how Sean Ellis was inspired both by the fierceness of contemporary fashion, by designers such as McQueen and Chalayan, and by the imagery of horror films. The fashion photographer Eugenio Recuenco is also well known in Europe for his haunting gothic narratives. Fashion spreads, such as "Les Costumes" for *Madame Figaro* magazine (2006) are lush, cinematic images of beauty and terror, inspired by gothic stories such as *Frankenstein*. According to Catherine Spooner: "Within gothic discourse, the clothes are the life: gothic chic is not a false surface for the gothic psyche, but an intrinsic part of it. Surely, therefore, within the world of fashion, it is this enduring potency of gothic images for imaginative self-identification that leads to their perennial revival."[97]

129. (left) *Amelia*, Steam Punk illustration, 2007. Illustration courtesy Freya Horn. www.artbyfreya.co.uk

130. (center) *Rufus*, Steam Punk illustration, 2007. Illustration courtesy Freya Horn. www.artbyfreya.co.uk

131. (right) J. Smith Esquire, Tattooed Top Hat, 2007. Silver, pig parchment, and watercolour ink, with leather thong silver frame made by Samson Steel; tattoo painted by Nikole Lowe. Photograph courtesy Justin Smith.

132. (facing page) Untitled from "Les Costumes," *Madame Figaro*, 2006. Photograph courtesy Eugenio Recuenco, represented by Gianfranco Meza & Co.

132. (following page) Untitled from "Les Costumes," *Madame Figaro*, 2006. Photograph courtesy Eugenio Recuenco, represented by Gianfranco Meza & Co.

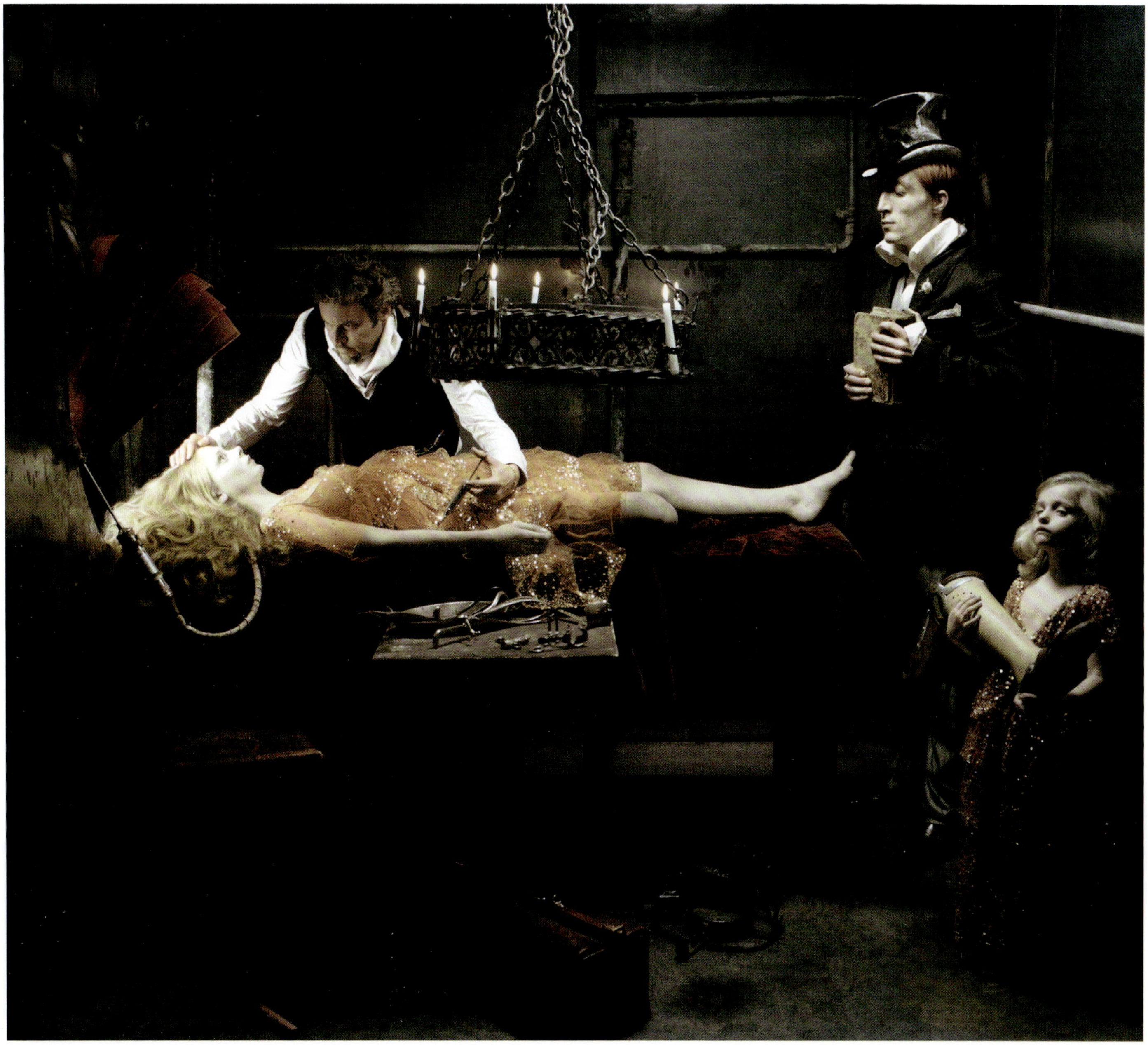

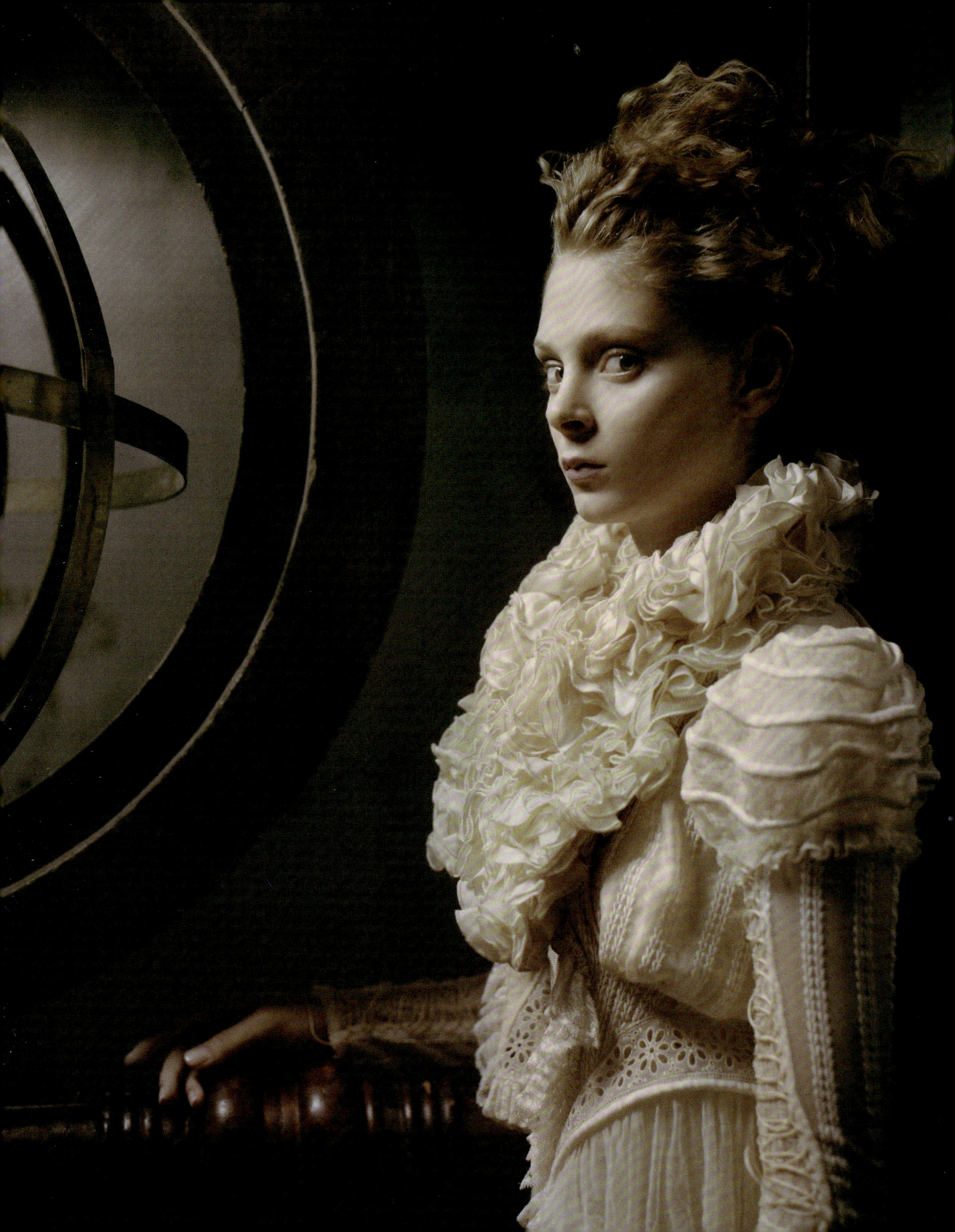

notes to gothic: dark glamour

1. Edmund Burke quoted in Richard Davenport-Hines, *Gothic: Four Hundred Years of Excess Horror, Evil, and Ruin* (New York: Farrar, Straus and Giroux, 1998), 1.

2. "Goth," *Fashion Rocks*, supplement to *Vogue* (September 2007).

3. Catherine Spooner, *Fashioning Gothic Bodies* (Manchester University Press, 2004): 1.

4. Henry Fuseli quoted in Davenport-Hines, *Gothic*, 236.

5. Sigmund Freud, *The Standard Edition of the Complete Psychological Works of Sigmund Freud*, vol. 17: *1917–1919* (London: Hogarth Press and the Institute for Psycho-Analysis, 1955), 233, 247–8.

6. Ibid., 241.

7. Horace Walpole, *Letters* (Whitefish: Kessinger Publishing, 2004), January 10, 1750.

8. Lord Macaulay, "Horace Walpole," *Edinburgh Review* (October 1833), cited in Timothy Mowl, *Horace Walpole: The Great Outsider* (London: John Murray, 1996), 255.

9. Walpole quoted in Christopher Frayling, Martin Myrone, and Marina Warner, *Gothic Nightmares: Fuseli, Blake and the Romantic Imagination* (London: Tate Publishing, 2006), 13.

10. Kenneth Clark, *The Gothic Revival: An Essay in Taste* (London: John Murray; New York: Holt, Rinehart & Winston, 1962), 42-43.

11. John Evelyn quoted in Davenport-Hines, *Gothic*, 2.

12. Horace Walpole, *Anecdotes of Painting*, quoted in Clark, *Gothic Revival*, 43.

13. Walpole, *Letters*, April 27, 1753.

14. Ibid., June 12, 1753.

15. Ibid., October 17, 1794.

16. Ibid., May 11, 1769.

17. Ibid., March 9, 1765.

18. Marquis de Sade, *Crimes of Love* (1800), quoted in Varma Devemdra, *The Gothic Flame* (London: Arthur Barker, 1957), 217.

19. Bram Stoker, *Dracula* (New York, Barnes & Noble, 1996), 40–41.

melancholy and the macabre

Gothic Rock and Fashion

Jennifer Park

bauhaus

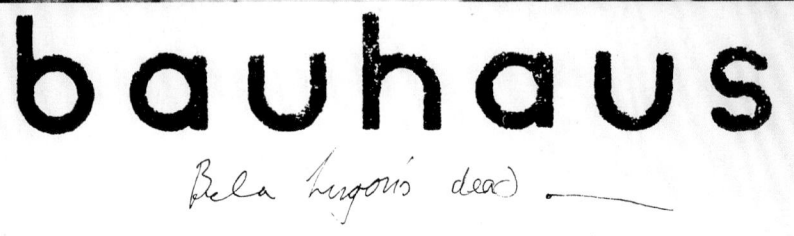

Bela Lugosi's dead

The virginal brides file past his tomb
Strewn with time's dead flowers
Bereft in deathly bloom
Alone in a darkened room
The count
Bela Lugosi's Dead
Undead undead undead[1]

In 1979 Bauhaus declared *Bela Lugosi's Dead*, and so heralded the unwitting birth of gothic rock proper. Released as a 12″ single, the original sleeve art included a film still taken from the German Expressionist masterpiece *The Cabinet of Dr. Caligari* (1920). The haunting image of the demented sleepwalking killer, culled from cinema's first modern horror flick, not only served to symbolize the brooding persona of Bauhaus, but irrevocably sealed the band's goth fate. Heavily made-up androgynous bodies clad in provocative all-black ensembles performed live renditions of the track as theater – complete with coffin (provided the venue allowed) and smoke machine, which generated an ominous fog that was then pierced by the gig's requisite stark strobe lighting. With the front man Peter Murphy's deep, hypnotic vocals layered over Danny Ash's experimental guitar noise, David J's haunting basslines, and Kevin Haskins's tribal drumming, Bauhaus audaciously personified the new dark direction in music that had come on the heels of the post-punk revolution already set in motion by Joy Division and Siouxsie And The Banshees.

Gothic as applied to music originally described bands whose sound foregrounded moody atmospherics. In contrast to punk's unbridled energy, fueled by discordant guitars and dissident vocals, what later came to be known as goth tended instead to focus on gloomy, introspective lyrics augmented by the melodic beat of a pounding bass guitar. Gothic rock also employed synthesizers and other modulated effects

1. Bauhaus, *Bela Lugosi's Dead*, 12″ single, front cover and back cover, Small Wonder, 1979. Courtesy Bauhaus.

set the fashion. It was only a matter of time before they took their street theatre to the stage."[14] For many post-punk groups who were on the verge of forming, the Sex Pistols provided the necessary catalyst to jolt them into action. The nascent Banshees were no exception. The Banshees' bassist Steven Severin later recalled, "After seeing the Pistols, I thought, 'This is it, this is our mission.'"[15]

Susan Janet Ballion (Siouxsie Sioux) and Steven Bailey (Steven Severin) grew up on the outskirts of London and sought refuge in music and fashion early on.[16] These two founding members of the Banshees were both Bowie fans. In describing the massive impact that glam rock had on her, Siouxsie Sioux stated, "It was the first time I felt that it was music made for me."[17] She went on to explain Bowie's significance:

> Bowie was incredible – the skinniness, the alienation, the otherworldliness. He was more than simply androgynous, though for the first time, I heard words such as "unisex" and "bisexual." I thought that was really interesting. He was aimed at both male and female audiences, and projected something very different to what most boys and girls were trying to conform to. It was definitely the man/woman of the future, and although nothing was ever said, you understood it instinctively, just by the imagery and the sounds that he used. It was about tearing down the old traditions and clichés. It was a brave new world, a springboard to accentuate your own individuality.[18]

Bowie moved past the music to articulate social currents seeping into youth culture by using the stage as a platform. He spoke directly to the next generation. Bowie's genderless "brave new world" preached that the infinite possibilities of the future could only surface in disavowing the past. Moreover, being "different" was not only all right, it was its own path to enlightenment. For self-professed freaks like Siouxsie Sioux, the message was messianic.[19]

Sioux's distinctive image evolved as she became a regular on the London club scene. Her identity was established through her imaginative ensembles and her creative use of make-up – all directly inspired by Bowie's legacy. She frequented Biba on Kensington High Street as a teenager and could even remember her first outfit by the label. A black-and-gold Chinese-inspired dress with a provocative, long side slit was the first of many Asian influences on Sioux's clothes.[20] Barbara Hulanicki's retro designs for Biba often referenced Art Nouveau. Appropriately, the designer's palette included dark, muted hues of plums, rusts, and berries. Traces of the existing Art Nouveau revival – epitomized by Biba's iconic logo of black-and-gold curvilinear lines – surfaced in later Banshees album art. For the band's fifth studio album, *A Kiss in the Dreamhouse* (1982), for example, the cover was inspired by the work of the Viennese Art Nouveau master Gustav Klimt. Klimt's exploration of allegory and his provocative depiction of overt sexuality not only resonated with many of the themes contained in the Banshees's introspective songs, it materialized in Sioux's own wardrobe.

By the time she met Severin, Sioux was a seasoned club kid. Severin, in contrast, came from more of a live-music scene. The Sex Pistols had begun a residency at the 100 Club on Oxford Street in London, where Severin was a loyal attendee. Sioux

12. Siouxsie Sioux at the Vortex Club, London, Summer 1977. Photograph courtesy Mick Mercer.

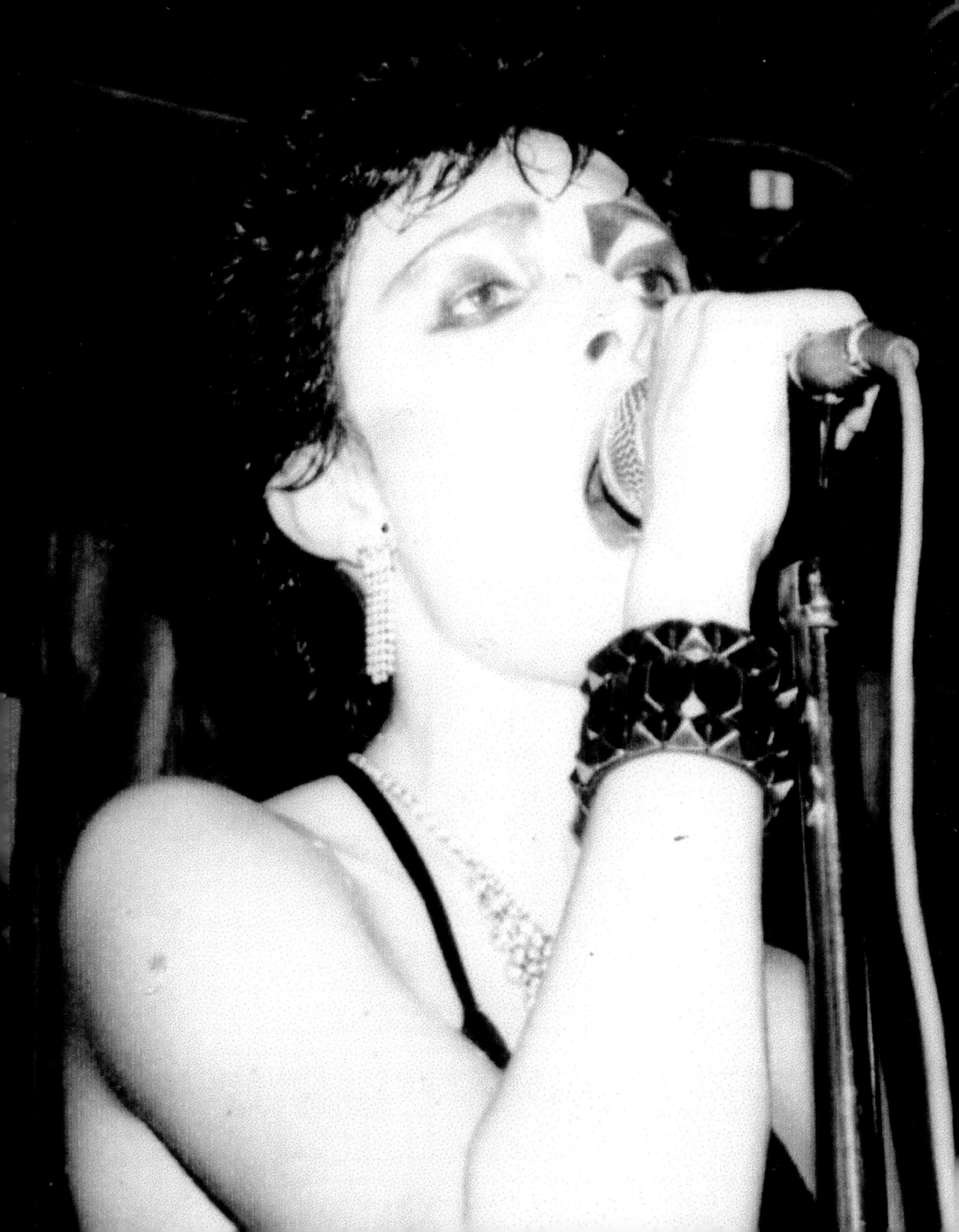

started going to the gigs and quickly made the connection between the Pistols and Vivienne Westwood and Malcolm McLaren. Their shop Sex, on the King's Road, sold fetish-influenced clothes and was a notorious punk-rock hangout. The store's wares, however, were not necessarily meant for punk's paupers, and, as Severin explained, "We never got to wear any of the clothes. Only those with rich parents could afford Sex clothes – that's when all the home-made thing started."[21] The Bromley Contingent's brand of do-it-yourself borrowed from fetish gear, mixed it up with diverse retro references, and injected punk paraphernalia. The initial stirrings of goth had appeared.

Although they never classified themselves as goth – and would even go so far as to actively repudiate the label – Siouxsie And The Banshees were instrumental in creating the goth genre. Legions of suburban Siouxsie Sioux clones around the world who identify as goths directly testify to this. In terms of dress, the Banshees' choice of fashion reaffirmed what they initially denied. From Sioux's early punk flirtation with Nazi chic *à la* swastika (which she repeatedly claimed was solely an act of provocation) through to the band's mature, doomy romanticized image, the Banshees' sartorial history continually serves as a major source of inspiration for goth subculture.

Significantly, the band's style contributed to the break with punk. By choosing a decidedly "un-punk" first album cover in *The Scream* (1978), the Banshees announced the arrival of dark glamour. Severin explained:

> The album deliberately had a completely un-punk sleeve. We had no intention of using blackmail writing like the Pistols. We wanted something clean and stark that matched the look of the band. At the time, we all wore black. Siouxsie would wear an occasional flash of white or blue, but that was all.

13. (left) Siouxsie And The Banshees, *A Kiss in the Dreamhouse*, cover, Polydor, 1982. Courtesy Universal Music Group.

14. (right) Siouxsie And The Banshees, *The Scream*, cover, Polydor, 1978. Courtesy Universal Music Group.

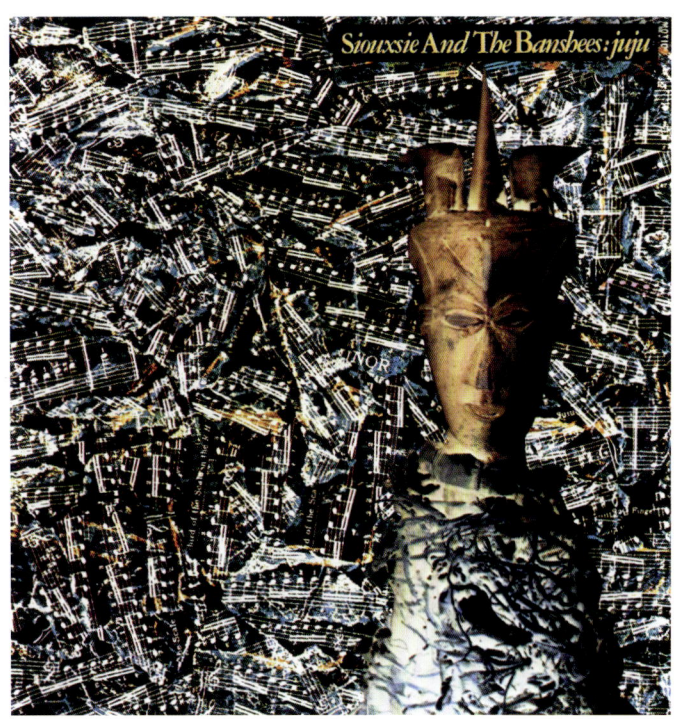

No other colors were allowed. I liked the kind of Beat thing about wearing black. It was the way The Velvets had dressed and I always thought that looked great. It's a very common look now, but back then it was unusual and set us apart from anyone else.[22]

Sioux personified this new dark, exotic glamour characteristic of would-be goth in her black, crimped, and teased-out hair; in her pale face and exaggerated Kabuki-like make-up; and in fashion that pulled together disparate influences, from non-western cultures to Victoriana and Deco to bondage and cabaret. Her unflinching, original style was documented in the live concert video *Nocturne* (1983), which was shot at the Royal Albert Hall in London. In a commanding voice, Sioux wails the opening track "Israel"; she has darkened, kohl-rimmed eyes and bright red lipstick. She wears a delicate deconstructed chiffon dress and accessories of costume jewels, black arm sheaths, and black leggings. Like the incarnation of an Otto Dix figure from a Weimar portrait, Siouxsie Sioux embodies the enigmatic torment characteristic of New Objectivity painting.

The band's rejection of the stigmatic goth label originates in a perceived bastardization of the term. Severin noted that at the time of the release of the band's second effort, *Join Hands* (1979), the Banshees themselves had described the album as "gothic."[23] In the making of the record they were influenced by nineteenth-century romantic literature, such as the works of Edgar Allan Poe: the track "Premature Burial," for instance, directly refers to Poe's short story of the same name.

Mirroring Poe's morbid tale, the Banshees' song ruminates on the line separating life from death. Is there choice in inevitability? What does futility *feel* like? Romanticism's emphasis on profound emotion was a reaction to the

15. (left) Siouxsie And The Banshees, *Join Hands*, cover, Polydor, 1979. Courtesy Universal Music Group.

16. (right) Siouxsie And The Banshees, *Juju*, cover, Polydor, 1981. Courtesy Universal Music Group.

scientific rationalism advocated during the Enlightenment. The gothic movement in its purest embodiment revived mysticism and unleashed an exploration of the Sublime by evoking such raw feelings as horror and awe. For Siouxsie And The Banshees, the connection to the gothic was rooted in the creation of songs that laid bare their mind's landscape. The Banshees hoped to tap into this particular aspect of the gothic rather than the "tacky harum scarum horror" often associated with the contemporary goth scene. Moreover, Severin later stated that he detested the goth categorization precisely "because most people don't even understand what that means."[24]

Juju (1981) was the Banshees' first concept album, and with such tracks as "Spellbound," "Arabian Knights," and "Voodoo Dolly," exoticism permeated the record. The sleeve artwork also reflected this. The band chose a reproduction of an African statue as the focus and placed it against a collaged background of torn pages of music all jumbled together. Although the band hated the goth label, *Juju* is widely considered the first proper album of the genre, both thematically and in its arrangement. It was a record copied by many later bands who actively called themselves goth. The Banshees often described their music as a cross between the drone of The Velvet Underground and the suspense of Alfred Hitchcock. When discussing *Juju* Sioux declared, "I've always thought that one of our greatest strengths was our ability to craft tension in music and subject matter. *Juju* had a strong identity, which the Goth bands that came in our wake tried to mimic, but they simply ended up diluting it. They were using horror as the basis for stupid rock'n'roll pantomime."[25] *Juju* was a crowning effort that marked a cohesive maturity in the band's development. The Banshees had come a long way from their first gig in September 1976 at the 100 Club Punk Rock Festival where Siouxsie Sioux notoriously shouted the *Lord's Prayer* over a wall of cacophonous noise.

The original guitarist, John McKay, and the original drummer, Kenny Morris, had infamously abandoned the band in 1979 before their gig at the Capital Theatre in Aberdeen. By the third album, Peter Clarke (Budgie) had joined them on drums and percussion and became a permanent member of the group. Guitarists, however, would come and go as if through a revolving door. Included in the long line of successors were John McGeoch, Jon Klein of Specimen fame, and Robert Smith of The Cure.

The Cure was the support band for the Banshees during the *Join Hands* tour. Robert Smith served double duty as the frontman of The Cure and as the Banshees' guitarist after McKay had walked out. Smith was a great fan of Siouxsie And The Banshees and already knew many of the songs. He recalled the impact of playing with the band: "On stage that first night with The Banshees I was blown away by how powerful I felt playing that kind of music. It was so different to what we were doing with The Cure. Before that, I'd wanted us to be like The Buzzcocks or Elvis Costello, the punk Beatles. Being a Banshee for the rest of the tour really changed my attitude to what I was doing."[26] Throughout his career Robert Smith – like the Banshees – denied the goth label. Yet before they sold out stadiums and dominated the pop charts, The Cure duly contributed to goth's embryonic state – first in the music and then in the look.

17. The Cure, *Seventeen Seconds*, cover, Fiction, 1980. Courtesy Universal Music Group.

Sonically, The Cure built on the legacy of Joy Division. The band's second album *Seventeen Seconds* was released in April 1980, the month before Ian Curtis's suicide on May 18. As with Joy Division, The Cure cited Bowie's *Low* as a source of inspiration. In addition, Smith obsessed over Nick Drake's heartbreakingly poetic *Five Leaves Left* (1969). Joy Division's *Closer* went on sale in record shops several months after Curtis's death. On hearing *Closer* for the first time, Smith expressed his amazement: "I can't ever imagine making something as powerful as this. I thought I'd have to kill myself to make a convincing record."[27] Curtis's brooding voice and somber lyrics, enhanced by Hannett's atmospheric innovations, became the springboard for the early Cure sound.

The Cure began as a three-piece – Robert Smith on lead vocals and guitar, Laurence "Lol" Tolhurst on drums, and Michael Dempsey on bass. The band signed to Polydor's independent label, Fiction, which was founded by the A&R man Chris Parry, who had also signed Siouxsie And The Banshees to Polydor.[28] Parry described his production concept for the band: "I wanted to make it totally different, elusive, translucent, stripped right down to the bones. I liked the lyrics and I liked Robert's voice and I was convinced, after the punk thrash, that people would want something more mysterious."[29] This recipe proved a success with the band's first single *Killing an Arab* (1978). Inspired by Albert Camus's *The Stranger* (1942), the track's acoustic sparseness revealed a bass-driven melody punctuated used to turn up wearing any sort of trousers and shoes, a white shirt, and a bit of a beard and I thought "These guys are the dog's breakfast! The music is great but they look shit."[35]

20. Bauhaus, 1980. Courtesy Beggars Banquet.

Transforming the band's schoolboy image was instrumental in transmitting the music's complete package. Not until Smith traded in his clean-cut look and innocent high-waisted pants and plain T-shirts did The Cure achieve global market penetration. Music videos by Tim Pope disseminated their spidery web of macabre imagery, and perhaps more importantly, it showcased Smith's big hair, make-up, and black wardrobe to millions of wayward suburban teenagers tuned into Music Television (MTV) and hungry to subsume an "alternative" dark identity. In their eyes it was goth, and for them it stood as a ready-made challenge to societal – not to mention parental – conventions.

Bauhaus, in contrast, was a band that understood the power of image early on. By 1979, when they released their stunning first single *Bela Lugosi's Dead*, the band already had a full-blown identity. Bauhaus was branded by their lowercase logo in similar typography to that of the eponymous school's name that adorned the entrance in Dessau, Germany, in the 1920s and 1930s, along with the abstract face icon once found on the institution's membership cards. The band was not naïve about this: they were aware of the movement's associations and translated its visionary ideals into a music revolution of their own. They gained notoriety through mesmerizing live gigs that showcased the band's theater-like performances. Following in the footsteps of their idols David Bowie and Iggy Pop, their frontman, Peter Murphy, commanded the stage in costume and make-up while belligerently challenging the audience. Bauhaus's biographer, Ian Shirley, remarked of Murphy: "He was a live wire; angry, vicious and totally commanding. He would actually attack the front few rows of people – in fact in the early days he picked up two convictions for GBH [grievous bodily harm] for assaulting members of the audience."[36] All this intensity was the reincarnation of the manifesto *Theatre of Cruelty (1938)* by the French poet and playwright Antonin Artaud. Artaud believed in sensory overload: theater meant nothing if it did not have a basic, overwhelming impact on the audience. In addition to grotesque or morbid content, Artaud utilized unusual sound and light in his performances in an effort to shock people and shatter any line separating their sphere of reality from the act on stage. He called this absolute freedom. Like their surrealist muse, Bauhaus insisted on the Artaudian concept of "culture-in-action"[37] – not only did the band explore taboo subjects in song, but their live gigs were experiments in bringing that message directly and confrontationally to the public.

The band was not content merely to play music: they had a vision for its reception and took pains to ensure its preservation. Their shows were calculated productions that included sparse lighting that created the perfect, sinister atmosphere to complement Murphy's choreographed, menacing movements to the band's ominous sounding tracks. "Mood lighting" additionally presented a dramatic backdrop to their sartorial choices. From fetish ensembles to elegant tuxedos, all became a standard for the goth genre. The erotically androgynous good looks of Peter Murphy and of the guitarist Danny Ash well suited the goth emphasis on

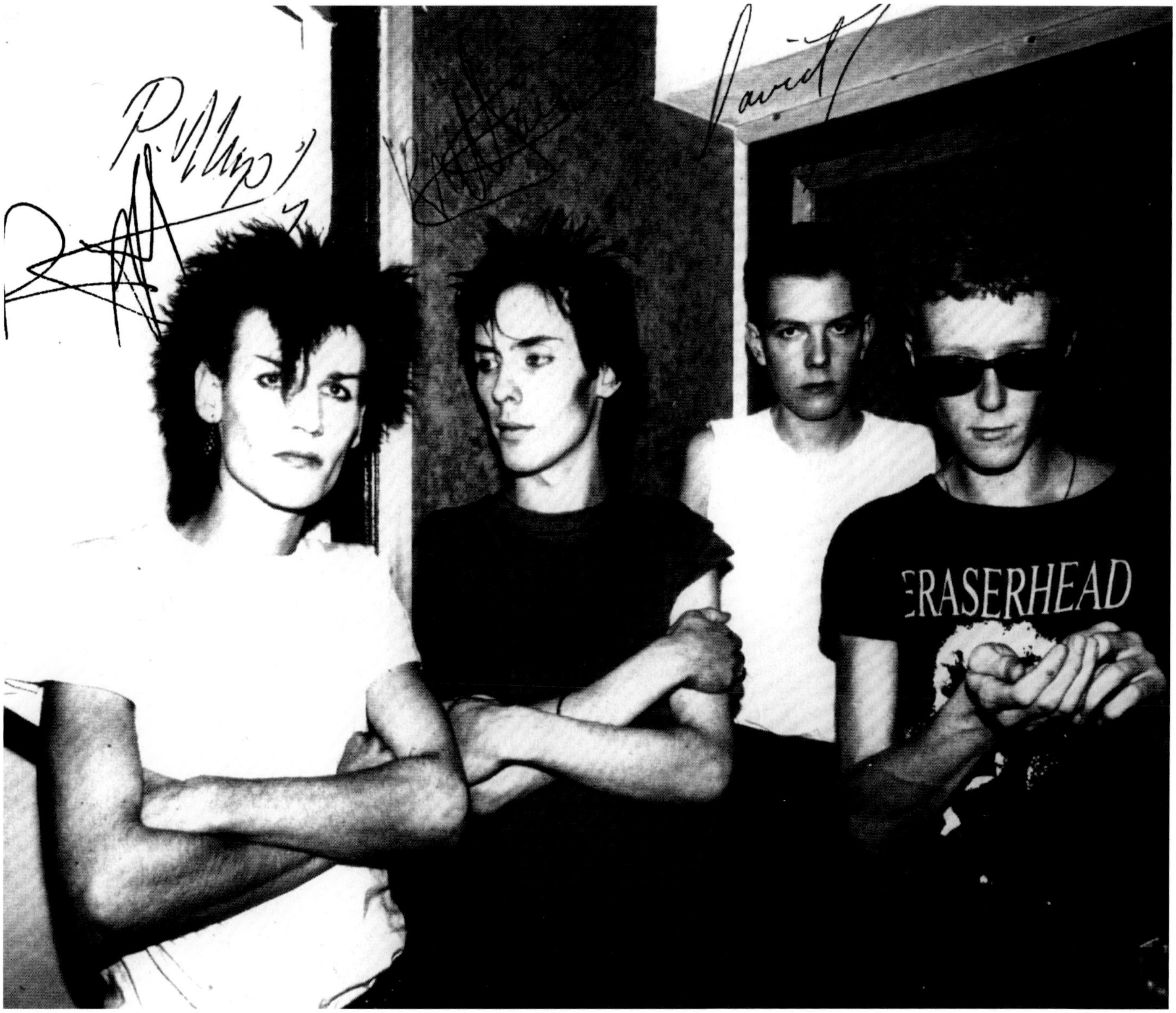
ERASERHEAD

21. Peter Murphy performing with Bauhaus at the Rock Garden, London, 1980. Photograph courtesy Mick Mercer.

beauty, and their attention to style again reiterated fashion's ultimate status in goth subculture. In becoming fashion icons, they inevitably provided a benchmark delineating goth. For example, Barry Briggs, the Sisters of Mercy online forum creator and self-professed goth, recalled his earliest incarnation: "I went through various styles of goth dress, the first one being what I guess you would call a Pete Murphy/Bauhaus look – dinner jacket, wing-tipped collar shirts (with tails), skin-tight black jeans and pointy boots, with long black hair worn either long and down or backcombed in a Danny Ash style."[38]

Bauhaus also used the emerging music video vehicle to consolidate their "gothic" image. Their second LP, *Mask* (1981), was released on the Beggars Banquet record label, later known for a roster that included many goth acts. The band made a video for the title track "Mask," for which the chosen time and location set the mood. Filmed at night in a rundown building, members of the band, clad in black, wander aimlessly in the decayed edifice before encountering Murphy's body covered in gray ashes. After paying their last respects, Murphy is resurrected. *Mask* is irrefutable evidence that Bauhaus pioneered the dark theatrics characteristic of the goth genre.

Then there was the music. Throughout their career, Bauhaus had a precarious relationship with the music press which often accused them of pretension. It all began with *Bela*. At more than nine minutes long, it was initially difficult to sell as a single for an unsigned band, but Bauhaus's uncompromising artistic exploration won and found enthusiastic ears at the independent label Small Wonder. On its release, the track received crucial airplay on John Peel's immensely influential evening show on BBC Radio 1, the network's pop station. With the debut of the original show, *Night Ride*, Peel declared, "This is the first of a new series of programmes on which you may hear just about anything."[39] Indeed, Peel was responsible for introducing once radical and obscure genres such as punk and reggae to BBC listeners, who were as passionate and eager as he to discover "something that was going to shake things up a bit."⁴⁰ Peel was probably the single most authoritative voice on new music at the time, and, for bands just starting out, the show was an important legitimizing platform that broadcast to an audience of enlightened music-lovers, some of whom became prominent musicians themselves.

Bela was a testament to the "atmosphere" that became a hallmark of gothic rock. The track incorporated Hannett's traditional rock-formula reversal and foregrounded David J's powerful bass lines and Kevin Haskins's forceful drumming. Murphy's deep, baritone voice sang the eulogy to Count Dracula incarnate in a deliberate, suspenseful manner that exuded a foreboding quality associated with the delivery of many later goth acts. Lyrically, the band consistently chose dark themes that flirted with religion and death, as exemplified by tracks such as "Stigmata Martyr" and "Exquisite Corpse."⁴¹ As they progressed, Bauhaus went a step further in the evolution of gothic rock and paved the way for the next generation by reinserting the "rock" dusted off from glam's legacy, courtesy of Ash's guitar work.

Ash's scathing guitar was featured in tracks such as "The Passion of Lovers."⁴² To support the single, Bauhaus went on a short tour with The Birthday Party as the support band. Surpassing even Bauhaus's intensity on stage, The Birthday Party, fronted by Nick Cave, stormed London's post-punk scene by unleashing unfettered aggression, the likes of which had not been seen since the literal climax of Iggy Pop's "lust for life." Their independent-chart-topping single *Release the Bats* (1981) was a sonic explosion of camp horror attack.⁴³ The band's high-energy live gigs directly inspired the first wave of goth bands, and the *New Musical Express* (NME) proclaimed on December 25, 1982 that "The Party have been indirectly

22. (left) Bauhaus, *Mask*, cover, Beggars Banquet, 1981. Courtesy Beggars Banquet.

23. (right) Bauhaus, *In the Flat Field,* cover, 4AD, 1980. Courtesy Beggars Banquet.

24. (top) Bauhaus, *The Sky's Gone Out*, cover, Beggars Banquet, 1982. Courtesy Beggars Banquet.

25. (bottom) Bauhaus, *Burning from the Inside*, cover, Beggars Banquet, 1983. Courtesy Beggars Banquet.

held responsible for the rise of a visceral new hardcore, ranging from The Sex Gang Children, through Danse Society to March Violets."

Hailing from Australia, The Birthday Party was a self-proclaimedly conceptual statement that probed even deeper into religious imagery, albeit in their own demented way. If goth subculture later obsessed over all things spiritual – from crucifixes to the occult – The Birthday Party offered up the most comprehensive and disturbing oeuvre on which it could ever draw. Records such as *Prayers on Fire* (1981), *Drunk on the Pope's Blood* (1982), and *Mutiny* (1983) captured The Birthday Party's raw, primal music that was steeped in religious retribution. The music video for the single *Nick the Stripper* (1981) opens a window into the dementia. It begins with a shot of the band's voodoo skull logo that fades into a carnival tent where

26. The Birthday Party, *Drunk on the Pope's Blood*, cover, 4AD, 1982. Courtesy Beggars Banquet.

30. The Sisters of Mercy, *Floodland*, cover, Merciful Release, 1987. Courtesy Warner Bros. Records Inc.

between members, compounded by Eldritch's well-documented controlling persona, made for salacious fodder which the music press easily converted into splashy headlines. Complicating the Sisters' desire to be judged on musical merits alone was their obvious infatuation with fashion and image. Eldritch's skeletal, amphetamine-fed body was the perfect clothes-hanger for rock style. Rarely spotted without his mirrored aviator sunglasses, he wore a uniform of head-to-toe black: black leather jacket and pants, black biker boots, black crushed western-style hat with floppy brim, and even black gloves. Moreover, in many respects the choice of Patricia Morrison as bassist – beginning with her work on *Floodland* (1987) – was not a decision made without weighing its aesthetic value. Music videos and promotional photographs showcased the perfect goth pin-up girl with her high arched eyebrows, black eyeliner, blood-red lips, teased-out hair, long black nails, and fetish-meets-renaissance wardrobe.

Eldritch's own Merciful Release label put out all the Sisters' records. By creating his own record label, Eldritch was able to control all aspects of production, from music making to sleeve design to marketing. The artwork for the Sisters' albums recalled the influence of Peter Saville's minimalistic design for Joy Division's *Unknown Pleasures*. A poetic image, the band's name, and the album title appear on covers, and the reverse side reveals only the track names, the Merciful Release logo (consisting of a human head – an image borrowed from *Gray's Anatomy* – embedded in a star), and the catalogue number. Not only was a record label the

31. The March Violets, *Crow Baby*, cover, 7″ single, Rebirth, 1983. Courtesy Rebirth Records.

perfect site for someone with such an unwavering artistic will, but, additionally, it allowed Eldritch to play a role in releasing music he thought was relevant. Merciful Release's first signing was The March Violets. Formed in 1981, the group's original line-up consisted of Simon D. and Rosie Garland on vocals, Tom Ashton on guitar, and Laurence Elliott on bass (in addition to his being the drum programmer). Influenced by groups like Gang of Four, The Birthday Party, and Bauhaus, The March Violets' sound was a more aggressive version of the Sisters' brand of droning rock. Again, the name of the band was chosen for its double meaning: March Violets evoked beautiful flowers, and at the same time it stood for the name that old-school Nazi Party members gave to new Nazi Party applicants who arrived only after Hitler's complete consolidation of power.

According to the Sisters' biographer, Andrew Pinnell, "The Violets were initially more successful than The Sisters and their first single, a four track EP featuring "Religious As Hell," "Fodder," "Children On Stun," and "Bon Bon Babies" became the first Merciful Release record to enter the Independent Single Chart in August 1982."[48] However, the relationship between the band and Eldritch did not last, and the Sisters' frontman threw the band off the label the following year. In response, The Violets followed in the footsteps of Eldritch and created their own record label appropriately titled Rebirth. Cleo Murray eventually replaced Garland, and with the band's cameo performance in the film *Some Kind* of *Wonderful* (1987), The Violets confirmed the depths to which gothic rock had penetrated popular culture.

The Violets supported The Danse Society on their tour of the U.K. in 1983. Like The Violets, The Danse Society was considered part of the first true wave of gothic rock bands. As their name implied, The Danse Society produced tracks with a strong beat. Songs from their first major-label LP, *Heaven is Waiting* (1984), revolved around spiritual matters and resembled a denser version of The Cure's more energized "Gothic Triptych" tracks. The androgynous good looks of their lead singer Steve Rawlings and his stylishly "romantic" clothes contributed to the band's overall popularity.

If The Danse Society explored spirituality of the western variety, Southern Death Cult was inspired by Native American culture as once brought to life – at least sartorially – by Adam and the Ants. In fact, the band's name came from an Indian tribe from the Mississippi Delta region. The frontman Ian Astbury's mohawk, his feather-and-bone jewelry, and his Native American-inspired dance visually completed the imagery embedded in tracks like "Moya," which metaphorically spoke of the parallel destruction of contemporary culture and the Indian race.

The band's sound took tribal drumming to a new level, but it was apparently only a fad. In 1983 Astbury formed a new band with the guitarist Billy Duffy, first renamed Death Cult, and then The Cult. Shedding their goth overtones with each successive amendment to their name, The Cult ultimately found a home in hard rock.

32. (top, left) The Danse Society, *Heaven is Waiting*, cover, Arista, 1984. Courtesy Big Life Management.

33. (top, right) Paul Gilmartin and Steve Rawlings of The Danse Society in Covent Garden, London, Summer 1982. Photograph courtesy Mick Mercer.

34. (facing page, top) Southern Death Cult at the Zig Zag Club, London, July 15, 1982. Photograph courtesy Mick Mercer.

35. (facing page, bottom) The Sex Gang Children, 1983. Courtesy Sex Gang Children.

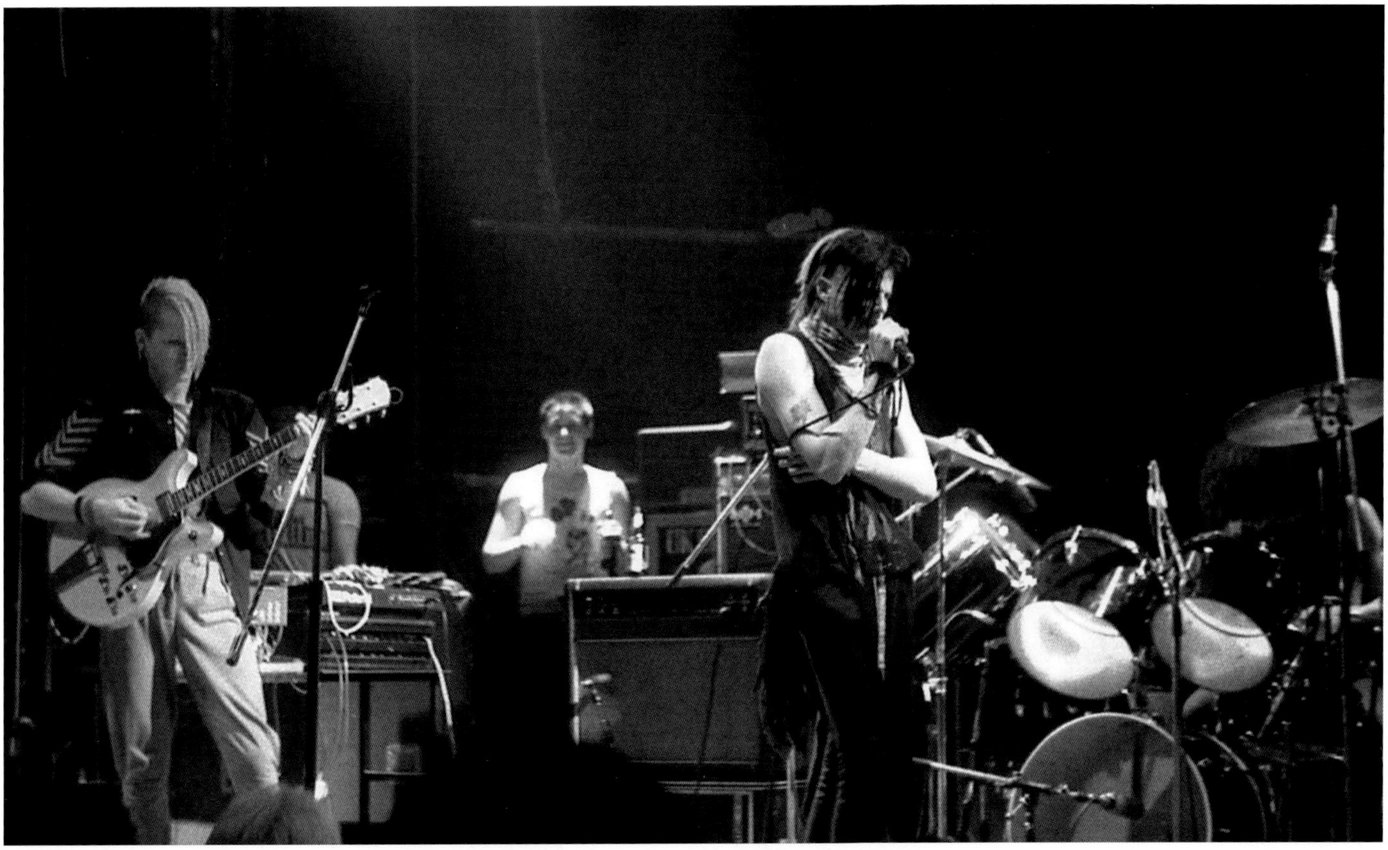

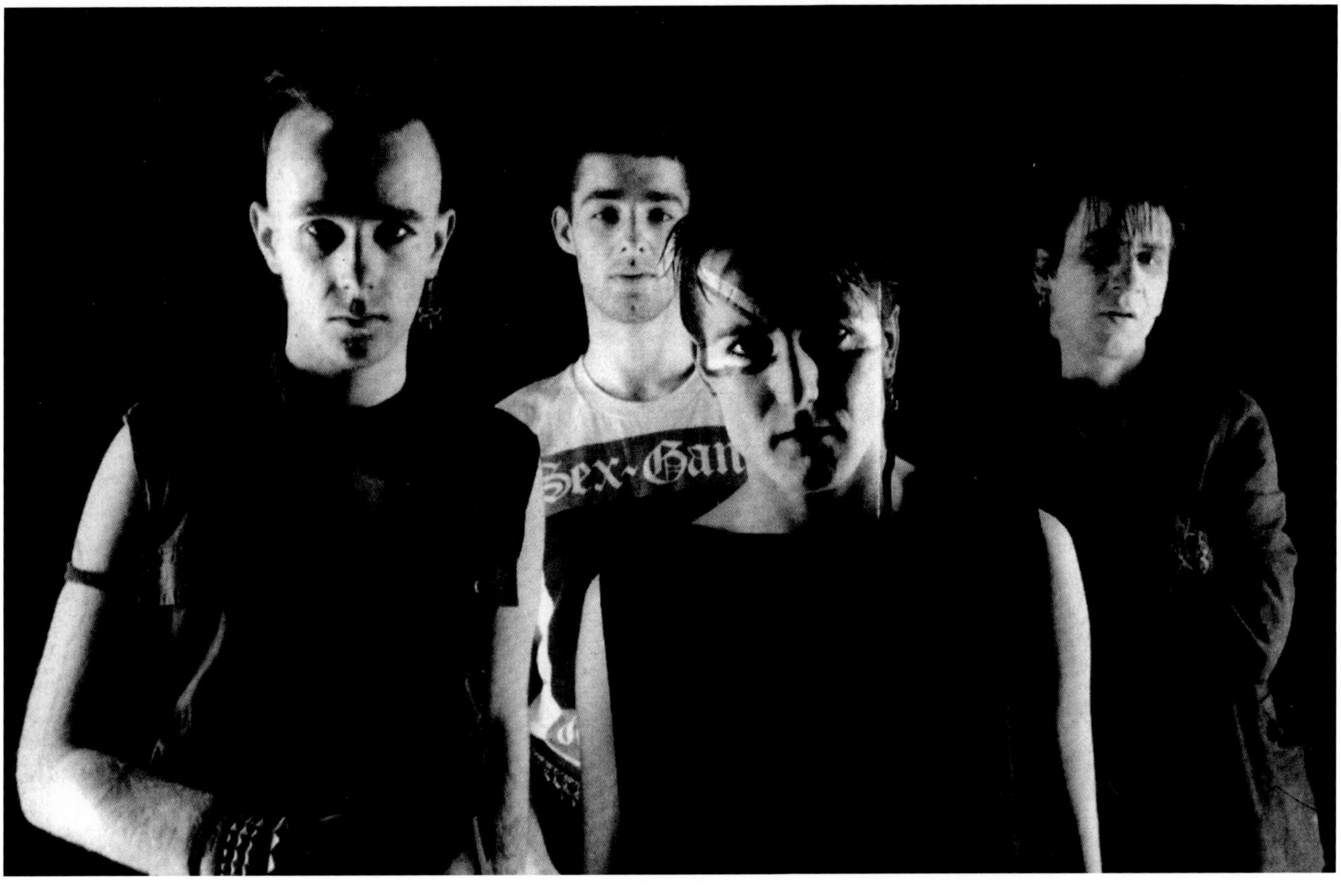
Sex-Gan

36. Sex Gang Children, *Naked*, cover, 1982. Recorded live at the Clarendon Ballroom. Courtesy Sex Gang Children.

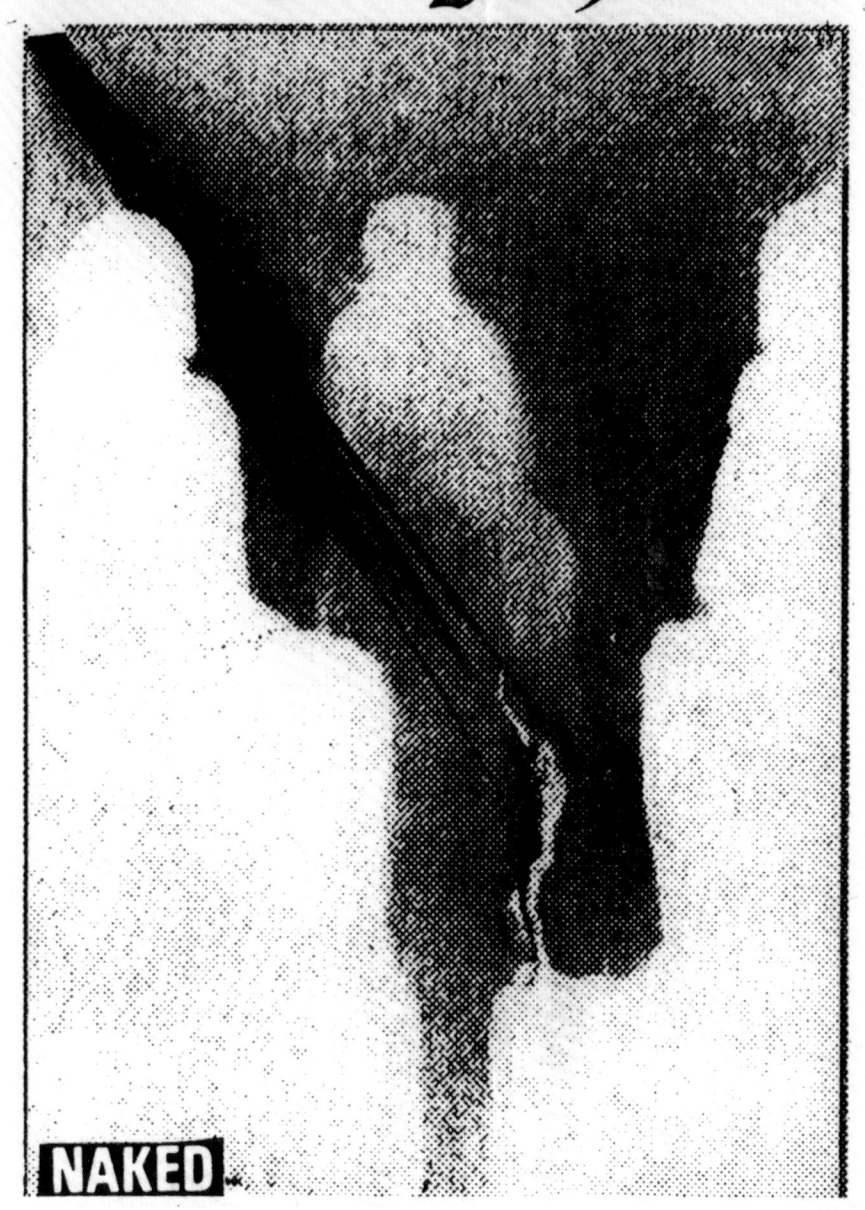

In November 1994, the *Alternative Press* magazine interviewed Ian Astbury and asked about his goth associations:

> The Goth tag was a bit of a joke, insists Ian Astbury. One of the groups coming up at the same time as us was Sex Gang Children, and Andi – he used to dress like a Banshees fan, and I used to call him the Goth Goblin because he was a little guy, and he's dark. He used to like Edith Piaf and this macabre music, and he lived in a building in Brixton called Visigoth Towers. So he was the little Gothic Goblin [...].[49]

The Sex Gang Children's version of gothic rock could best be described as creepy cabaret. The unique, high-pitched vocals of the frontman, Andi Sex Gang, were

37. Andi Sex Gang, *The Naked & the Dead*, cover, Revolver, 1986. Photograph: Claire Pollock. Courtesy Andi Sex Gang.

performed in a staccato-like manner against dramatic music that showcased Gothic Rock's usual sonic suspects: intense atmospherics, tribal drumming, pounding bass, and droning guitars. Live gigs shrouded in smoke effects provided the eerie aura the band so naturally projected. Andi Sex Gang's fashion, which merged the Bromley Contingent with camp horror, became a major influence on goth clubgoers during the Batcave era and beyond.

goth's disciples: dead and reburied

While the majority of gothic rock's founders have disbanded, their music lives on in countless club nights and in the host of contemporary bands that borrow directly from their legacy. Club culture plays an integral role in sustaining goth communities around the world. For goth it all began in 1982 with the Batcave, created by the band Specimen at the Gargoyle Club in London's Soho. It was originally conceived as "more of an arts space with [Specimen] as the host band and a diverse crowd of people [. . .] who were into music."[50] The lead singer of Specimen, Ollie Wisdom, scouted the location, which was a burlesque joint during the day and hosted the Batcave on Wednesday nights. In an interview with the goth magazine *Orkus* in 1997, the guitarist Jon Klein described the décor and general atmosphere: "Traveling up four floors in a tiny elevator, you passed through a coffin gateway into a well dressed labyrinth featuring a cinema/cabaret theater, hybrid disco, live music and an atmosphere of mid-week mayhem!"[51] Contemporary goth culture was undoubtedly formed here, and with the success of the club night, Specimen were able to export their little enclave of camp-horror cabaret at Batcave spin-offs around Britain, and even across the Atlantic at New York's Danceteria.

Specimen was a glam-camp band that cited Bowie's *Ziggy Stardust* and Reed's *Transformer* as "deep influences."[52] The original line-up included Ollie Wisdom on vocals, Jon Klein on guitar, and Kev Mills on bass. Jonny Melton (Jonny Slut), who in time became the face of the band, joined in 1982 on keyboards after being scouted one night at the Batcave. As he recounted to Mick Mercer, "First week I went to The Batcave I thought it was brilliant [. . .]; this disco that played Killing Joke and Bauhaus and Glam Rock. I went the second week and was approached by Ollie Wisdom who said, 'Do you want to join our band?' I said, 'Oh I can't

38. Audience at the Batcave, London, August 10, 1983. Photograph courtesy Mick Mercer.

play anything!' He said, 'That doesn't matter, you've got nice hair', gave me a telephone number and that was it really. I'd joined."[53] Jonny Slut's induction to the band validated the status of fashion in Specimen's take on nouveau glam. Goth seemingly reconciled itself with its obvious obsession. Either as performer or as civilian, "clothes had to be loud!"[54] Klein recounted, "We didn't dress down particularly during daylight, so it was always entertaining getting stopped by the police (one officer threatened to take me to the station on account of dangerous earrings!)."[55] While Klein preferred to "cannibalize stuff with scissors, liquid eyeliner, and paint,"[56] Wisdom borrowed from girlfriends' closets, and Slut relied on designer friends. Androgynous-punk-fetish-gore encapsulated the band's look of deathly pallor, make-up, and wardrobe of sinister black. As they mockingly questioned in the track "Beauty of Poison," "With your black, and your sack, and your leather anorak, do you feel . . . DARK?"[57] Specimen's dark twist reflected contemporary currents of horror pervasive in popular culture. When asked about

39. Dancers at the Batcave, London, August 10, 1983. Photograph courtesy Mick Mercer.

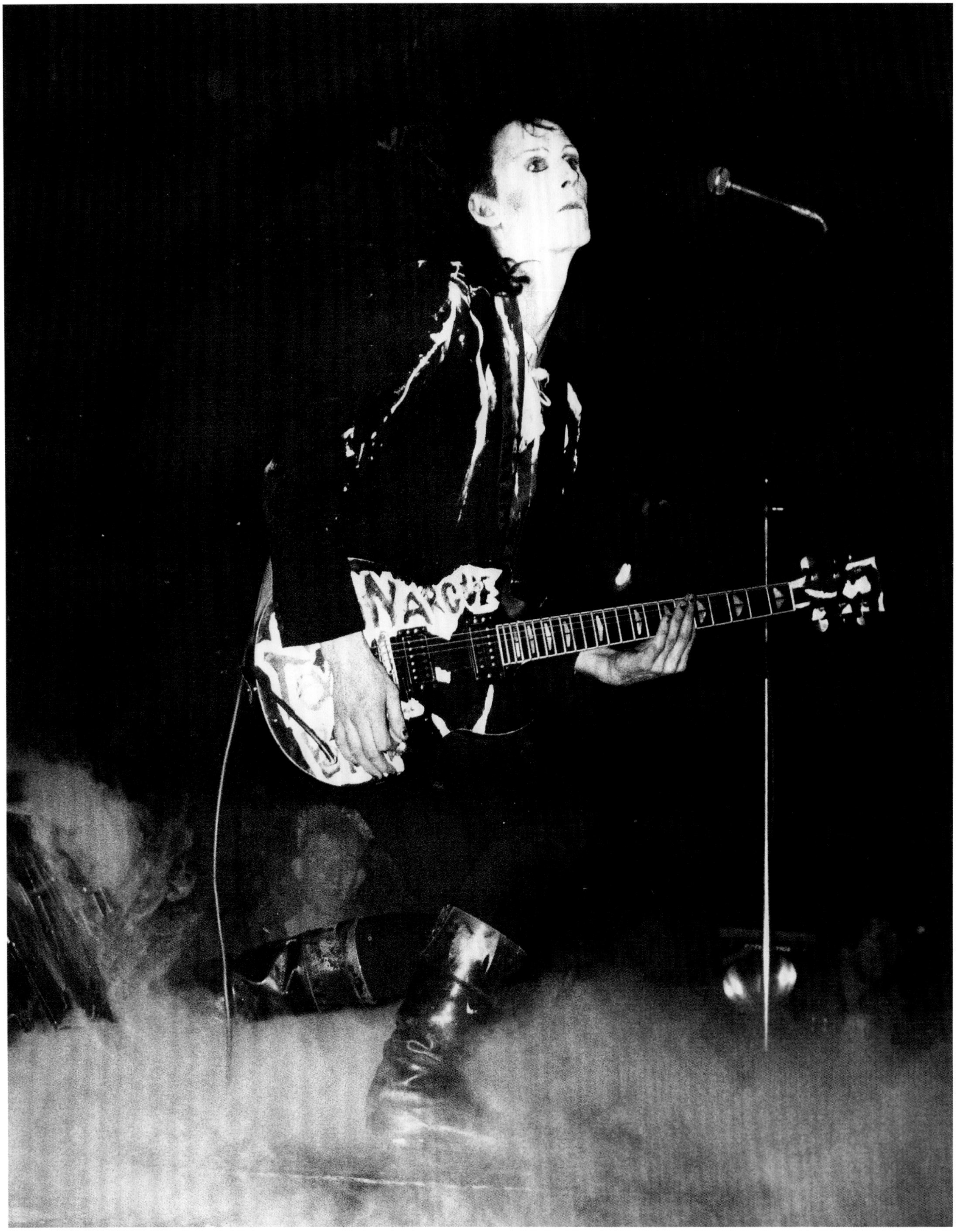

its impact on the band, Klein stated, "I guess it was in the air at the time. In cinema we had films like *The Evil Dead* (1981) and *Texas Chainsaw Massacre* (1974), in music Bauhaus had done *Bela Lugosi*, and the Banshees had made *Juju*. Once it started it took on it's own life..."[58]

Other goth acts such as Alien Sex Fiend also played at the Batcave in addition to the house band. Taking camp horror to a place where "people could neither believe their ears, or retrieve their eyes,"[59] Alien Sex Fiend's frontman, Nik Fiend, buttressed the grotesqueness cultivated in tracks such as "Wish I Woz A Dog," "I'm Not Mad," and "New Christian Music" from *Who's Been Sleeping in My Brain?* (1983) through his equally disturbing appearance and music delivery.

As with all clubs, the Batcave spun DJ sets with carefully curated tracks that in time became representative of goth. At the club's peak period (1982–83), Hamish Macdonald was resident DJ, and his mix included selections from punk, post-punk, glam, reggae, and electronica.[60] Long after the Batcave had been written into goth history, club nights that resurrected its aura crucially continued to disseminate the soundtrack for goth subculture by mixing in the classics. Moreover, music was not limited to straight gothic rock, but also incorporated post-punk influences and the mopey side of indie rock. The Smiths (and later a solo Morrissey), the Cocteau Twins, Echo and the Bunnymen, and The Jesus and Mary Chain are just a few of the non-gothic rock bands that can often be heard on many a goth night. Disparate musical influences cited by goth bands themselves point to the diverse sources of darkness in sound.

Not only did post-punk provide a fertile breeding ground for new melancholic music to flourish, it was also revolutionary in generating scores of independent record labels and distribution networks. Indie endeavors such as Factory Records, 4AD, and Rough Trade were all formed during this era. They were fronted by

40. (facing page) Jon Klein wearing his "Pigeonshit suit," 1983. Courtesy Jon Klein.

41. (top, left) Specimen, *Azoic*, front cover, Jungle, 1997. Courtesy Jon Klein.

42. (top, right) Specimen, *Azoic*, back cover, Jungle, 1997. Courtesy Jon Klein.

Spooner, Catherine 29, 105, 108
Steam Punk look 106–8, *107–8*
Steampunk Magazine 108
Stern 10
Stoker, Bram: *Dracula* 7, 18
Strawberry Hill, Middlesex 12, 14–15, *15*, 16
subcultures 3, 33, 43–4
   see also goth subculture
Sublime and gothic 11, 134
Sui, Anna 98, *98*
Sumner, Bernard 125, 127
supernatural themes 11, 16, 79, 80
Symphony of Shadows (shop) *37*, 40

Tattooed Top Hat *108*
Tear Dress 65
Technos 48
teenage subcultures *see* youth subcultures
Teese, Dita von *32*
Teller, Juergen 78
"terrorist chic" style 35
"terrorist" literature 13, 16, 18
Thaw, Joanna 74
Theatre of Cruelty 138
Theyskens, Olivier 3, 90–91, *90–91*, *93*, *104*
Thornton, Sarah 47
Tischi, Ricardo 88–9, *89*
Toledo, Ruben: "Midnight Angel" 60, *62*
transgressive practices 47, 78–9
Transylvania and vampire myth 18
Treacy, Philip *67*
True Grace England *7*, *41*
Twice the Siren *41*

UK Decay 35
"uncanny, the" 11–12

Vadukul, Max *19*
Valli, Giambattista *98*
vampires 18–23, 30, 96
   film costumes 18, *20–21*, *23*, 42
   and goth look 38
Vampyre Society *42*, 43
Vanian, Dave 38, *39*
Velvet Underground, The 118–20, *119*, 160

Victoria, Queen 24
Victorian fashion
   and goth subculture 37, 40, 42–3, 47, 105–6, *105*
   mourning dress 7, 22–5, *23–5*, 105
   and Steam Punk look 106–8, *107–8*
Vinken, Barbara 30, 33, 66, 68
Viollet-le-Duc, Eugène Emmanuel 15
Visigoths 4
Visionaire 19
visual-kei music in Japan 54, 57
Vlad the Impaler (Vlad Dracul) 18
Vogue magazines 7, 10, *17*, *32*, *62*

Walpole, Horace 12–15, *14*
   The Castle of Otranto 6, 12–13, 16
   Strawberry Hill 12, 14–15, *15*, 16
Warhol, Andy 119, *119*, 160
Wax Bodies (magazine) 68
Webb, Ryan 54
Wenchwear *46*
Westwood, Vivienne 33, 40, 132
Whitby, Yorkshire *42*, 43
white nightgown and vampire myths 11, *12*, *21*, *23*
widows and mourning dress 25, *25*
Wildgoose, Jane *106*
Willis, Ellen 119
Wilson, Tony 127
Wisdom, Ollie 151, *152*, 153
witchcraft: iconography of 80
Wolff, Bernard Pierre 127, *129*
women
   and dandyism 30, *32*, 33
   vampire costumes 18, *21*, *23*
Wright, Karen 42–3

Yamamoto, Yohji 3, 59, *64*, 66, 70–71, *72*, 99
Yeohlee (designer) 98–9
   Gothic Arch Dress 99, *99*
Yoshinaga, Masayuki *8*, 60–1
youth subcultures 3, 33, 43–4
   see also goth subculture

Ziggy Stardust And The Spiders From Mars (film) 121